NOT A DROP TO DRINK

NOT A DROP TO DRINK

AMERICA'S
WATER CRISIS

[AND WHAT YOU CAN DO]

KEN MIDKIFF

New World Library
Novato, California

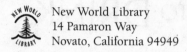 New World Library
14 Pamaron Way
Novato, California 94949

Cover design by Laura Beers
Interior design by Madonna Gauding

Library of Congress Cataloging-in-Publication Data
Midkiff, Kenneth.
Not a drop to drink : America's water crisis (and what you can do) / Ken Midkiff.
      p.   cm.
Includes bibliographical references and index.
ISBN 978-1-930722-68-2 (pbk. : alk. paper)
1. Water-supply–United States. 2. Water rights–United States. 3. Water consumption–United States. 4. Water resources development–United States.
I. Title.
TD223.M489 2007
363.6'10973–dc22   2007020953

First printing, June 2007
ISBN-10: 1-930722-68-0
ISBN-13: 978-1-930722-68-2
Printed in Canada on 100% postconsumer-waste recycled paper

g New World Library is a proud member of the Green Press Initiative.

10   9   8   7   6   5   4   3   2   1

This book is dedicated to my wife, Julie; my sons, Mike and Charlie; and my grandchildren, Simon, Eben, and Chloe.

May they always have water to drink.

CONTENTS

FOREWORD

The struggle over the world's water resources will be the defining struggle of the twenty-first century, and the battle has already been joined.

In 1999, following the advice of the World Bank, the Bolivian government allowed the city of Cochabamba in Bolivia to contract with a subsidiary of the Bechtel company to take over the city's public water supply. The company, composed primarily of British investors, immediately raised water rates, causing extreme hardship for all but the city's wealthiest citizens. The outcome, unexpected by Bechtel as well as the Bolivian government, was otherwise predictable: the public revolted against the rising rates. Massive street protests pitted rock-throwing mobs of Cochabamba's poor against riot police who maimed or killed them. This mini-revolution caused Bolivia's government to collapse and rescind the privatization of the city's water. Was this a communist mob bent on nationalizing legitimate private property? Hardly. Cochabamba's citizens were engaged in the most fundamental fight for democratic rights.

The best measure of how a democracy functions is how it distributes the goods of the land: the air, waters, wandering animals, fisheries, and public lands, otherwise known as the "public trust" or the "commons." By their nature these resources cannot be reduced to private property but are the shared assets of all the people, held in trust for future generations. Since ancient times, the laws of all just and equitable nations have protected these public trust assets as the property of all citizens, humble and noble, rich and poor alike; everyone has the right to use the commons in a way that does not diminish its use by others.

Ancient Roman law, our earliest legal heritage, held that the most fundamental "natural," or God-given, law required that the "air, running water, the sea, and consequently the sea shore" could not be owned as private property but were "common to all" Roman citizens.[1] The Romans vigorously protected the waterways and the resources of the sea, seashore, estuaries, wetlands, and fisheries from control by private individuals.

The first acts of a tyranny invariably include efforts to privatize the commons. Despotic governments typically allow favored persons or powerful entities to capture and consolidate the public trust and steal the commonwealth from the public.

Following Rome's collapse, Europe's kings and feudal lords appropriated public trust assets, including rivers and streams, and dispensed them without regard to public rights. In the early years of the thirteenth century, Britain's King John fenced in England's forests and streams, erected navigational tolls, and placed weirs in the rivers in order to sell private monopolies to the fisheries. The exclusion of the public from the rivers and waterways and the stifling of commerce that ensued helped prompt a citizens' revolt. In 1215 the English barons trounced King John at Runnymede and forced him to sign the Magna Carta, which guaranteed the personal liberties of the people of England. Centuries later the Magna Carta served as the blueprint for the Bill of Rights in the U.S. Constitution.

Among the rights reaffirmed by the Magna Carta were "liberty of navigation" and a "free fishery," so that, according to Britain's seminal legal authority, William Blackstone, "the rivers that were fenced [by the king] were directed to be laid open."[2] Subsequent court decisions interpreted the Magna

Carta to mean that "the King was trustee" holding public waters "as protector of public and common rights" and "he could not appropriate them to his own use."[3] Similarly, eleventh-century French law provided that "the running water and springs...are not to be held by lords...nor are they to be maintained...in any other way than that their people may always be able to use them."[4] Thirteenth-century Spanish law likewise ensured the public inalienable rights in rivers, springs, and shores.

Additionally, the king could not sell public trust assets to a private party. The nineteenth-century legal scholar Henry Schultes described public trust rights as "unalienable." He explained that "things which relate to the public good cannot be given, sold, or transferred by the King to another person."[5] Henry William Woolrych, another legal scholar of the period, added that "notwithstanding such a grant, if the public interest be invaded, or the privileges of the people narrowed, the grant, *pro tanto* is void."[6]

Following the American Revolution, each state became sovereign, inheriting from King George III the trusteeship of public land, waters, and wildlife within its borders. Both the federal government and the individual states recognized the public trust in their statutes and ordinances. For instance, Massachusetts's Great Pond Ordinance of 1641 assured public access to all consequential water bodies, and the federal government's Northwest Ordinance of 1787 gave all U.S. citizens unrestrained access to all the tributaries of the St. Lawrence and Mississippi rivers and proclaimed that those waters and "the carrying places between shall be common highways and forever free."[7]

Like the citizens of Great Britain in 1215, Cochabamba's citizens saw the privatization of the commons as a threat to their democracy and their lives. While privatization controversies in the United States have not yet provoked hot confrontations like those that occurred in Cochabamba, local public utilities across North America are even now conveying water supplies that have benefited from substantial public investment to private companies, often at fire-sale prices. In recent years, only vigorous protests by citizens have kept corporations from privatizing the water supplies in places like Lexington, Kentucky, and Stockton, California. Elsewhere, a more subtle but equally effective privatization of public trust waters is occurring, as governments subsidize reckless and unsustainable water usages that favor greedy developers, powerful utilities, and agribusiness barons over the American public. Ken Midkiff tells how destructive government policies are draining our nation's rivers and aquifers and trampling our democratic rights.

In the American West, the federal government provides oceans of money to corporate agribusiness to raise wasteful water-dependent crops like rice and alfalfa in the desert. Meanwhile, local and state governments encourage sprawling and water-hungry commercial and residential developments by offering tax breaks and by subsidizing infrastructure including roads, sewer lines, and electricity. With such inducements developers are building golf courses and swimming pools in the Arizona desert and draining the 112-million-acre, ten-million-year-old Ogallala Aquifer under the Great Plains states, which has dropped several hundred feet since modern irrigation practices surged following World War II. Similar uses have drained the Colorado River dry.

In 1967 my father took me and eight of my brothers and sisters on a Colorado River white-water trip through the Grand Canyon. The Glen Canyon Dam, just above our put-in, had been completed three years before, and Lake Powell was still filling. The new dam complemented the Hoover Dam nearly 300 miles downstream at the other end of the Grand Canyon. Together, they promised to irrigate a thirsty West, generate hydropower, and create great lakes with recreational opportunities for millions. But critics saw the Glen Canyon Dam as a wasteful and reckless boondoggle to corporate agriculture and greedy developers. Environmentalists said the dam would destroy the Grand Canyon National Park's unique ecology and that the lakes would lose horrendous amounts of water to evaporation and seepage and would soon fill with sediment.

That year we camped on the Colorado's massive sandbars and bathed and swam in her 70-degree water and caught some of the abundant schools of native fish. When I returned in 2006 to kayak the Grand Canyon with my daughter Kick, the spacious sandy beaches and massive driftwood piles where I camped with my father were gone. The river, which should be warm and muddy, was clear and a frigid 46 degrees. Four of the river's eight native fish species are extinct, with two others headed there soon. The beavers, otters, and muskrats have also disappeared, as have the indigenous insect species. Sediment has already flatlined hydropower and nearly choked the upper reaches of Lake Powell, which is in severe decline as a tourist destination. The Colorado River no longer reaches the sea or feeds the great estuaries in the Gulf of California that once teemed with life. Instead, it ignominiously dies in the Sonoran desert. What was once a dynamic and specialized ecosystem cutting through the greatest monument to America's national heritage has been transformed into a cold-water plumbing conduit between the two largest reservoirs in the United States — monuments to greed, shortsightedness, and corporate power.

The Colorado has been successfully hijacked by the water and power agencies who obstruct and control her waters to favor hydropower production over the river's management as a national park or her stunning ecological, historical, cultural, and recreational values.

And all the grave prophecies of the scientists and environmentalists have come true. The reservoirs are emptying because of human consumption, a situation now exacerbated by climate change. Lake Powell is now nearly 100 feet below its capacity level. Hydropower revenues for repayment to the U.S. Treasury have been at a standstill for six years. Recreational access at the upper reaches of Lake Mead and Lake Powell is now defunct because of the impact of sediment and fill. Water quality is dropping precipitously, and farmers need more water to flush the dissolved solids from their fields. The metropolitan growth and agribusiness consumption triggered by the dam's original promise continue at a rampant pace.

The Colorado River has nothing more to give, and a train wreck is imminent. But while scientists continue to sound the warning, the river managers insist on business as usual, encouraging wasteful agricultural uses, the proliferation of urban sprawl, and dramatic increases in consumption. It is a system geared to reward the powerful and impoverish the rest of us.

The Colorado River is the poster child for bad water management. But Midkiff shows how the Colorado River and its enabling infrastructure can be retooled to fit reality, benefit the commons, and comply with the intent of the law.

Midkiff shows that if the handouts ceased, we could easily meet today's needs while ensuring the uncompromised rights of our children. In order to succeed we must adopt a healthy socioeconomic system that rewards the efficient use of resources and punishes their inefficient use. Our legal system must confront polluters with the social costs of their activities. Midkiff discusses how we can implement rational water policy in the West that services America's citizens rather than the greedy powerful few and that creates an example for the democratic use of public trust resources worldwide.

But Americans need to be aware of their rights and the jeopardy corporate power places them in. Democracy affirms individual rights to our natural resources. But those rights cannot survive without a courageous citizenry that insists that its government not merely cater to commerce and industry but aggressively protect its citizenry's right to good health; safe air, water, and food; and the enrichment of America's national heritage and God's creation.

— Robert F. Kennedy, Jr.

INTRODUCTION

The Current State of Emergency
Facing the American Water Supply

D amn it! Another boil order! I wish that just for a few days what comes out of the tap wouldn't need to be boiled to be drinkable." That was the response of an Atlanta citizen I spoke with in 2002 after she received the third announcement in a week that tap water should be boiled before consumption.

Unfortunately, Atlanta's water crisis is not an isolated incident. Across the country — in rural areas served by public drinking-water utilities, in small towns, and in big cities like Atlanta — low water pressure has led to the possible contamination of tap water. As a result, more and more "boil orders" are being issued by drinking-water utilities and public health agencies.

This low water pressure, which in the past occurred only when water was shut off during repairs, is more and more the result of actual water shortages — a situation our water systems have not been designed to accommodate. When water pressure becomes low in underground pipes, the low pressure allows nasty stuff to get in the pipes. In the best of situations, all that results is muddy water. But in extreme cases, when harmful bacteria contaminate water, myriad health problems, including diarrhea, vomiting, organ damage, and prolonged illness, can come about if citizens drink the water coming out of their faucets.

As yet, there have been no confirmed deaths from this sort of waterborne contamination — but things are getting worse, not better. As this country runs short of water, it could well be that boil orders will be viewed as positive — at least water will be coming out of our taps. In many areas of the United States, there might not be any water at all, except what is for sale in the supermarket. Buying bottled water is expensive now and will without a doubt be more expensive in the future. In addition to the usual inflation, the spiking demand for water and the dwindling supply will increase the price per gallon astronomically. From the current rate of about $1 per gallon in plastic jugs, the cost is likely to reach $5 or more per gallon. Obviously, such costly water will be used only for essential purposes, mostly drinking and cooking. Such niceties as bathing and washing dishes will become luxuries that average citizens won't be able to enjoy on a regular basis or maybe at all.

Of course, a water shortage won't only affect the quality and amount of the water that comes into our homes; it will also likely result in a dramatically diminished food supply. Crops need water to grow. As the major agricultural centers of our nation dry up — which is already happening at an alarmingly rapid pace — we can expect both shortages of water- dependent food and a huge increase in the cost of produce, meats, and grains. Most foods could become so expensive that only the very wealthy will be able to eat well. It's conceivable that rice and potatoes could become the only reasonably priced foods available, making a balanced diet impossible for the vast majority of consumers.

When organizations such as the Union of Concerned Scientists and Public Citizen, as well as concerned health care providers, have expressed concern about our water and food supplies, they've been dismissively accused of being Chicken Littles. But their fears are justifiable. For people in many nations — Nigeria, India, Kenya, and even China — food shortages have led to diets of rice and little else. While it is unlikely that this country will face such shortages in the near future, a steadily declining abundance is certain.[1]

From Too Much to Too Little in One Century

When the United States was founded, there were vast acreages of wetlands. Land that today is taken up with the production of corn and soybeans in the central Midwest — Illinois, Indiana, Ohio, parts of Iowa, as well as the eastern portion of Kansas — was covered with water. In the 1900s, farmers in that area had to join together and dredge out rivers and streams, constructing drainage ditches to draw the water off the land and expose the rich soil. While yesterday's marshes are today's farmlands, little could those farmers have imagined that in 2006, those same fields would be in dire need of water and that wells that once produced water sufficient to nourish 160 acres would need to be dug deeper and deeper to produce water sufficient for half that acreage.[2]

As recently as the 1800s, the only problem our nation faced concerning water was having too much of it. People in the East faced flooding rivers. On the Oregon Trail, crossing streams and rivers posed a significant problem to pioneers headed west in wagon trains. Lives were lost, wagons and cargo got swept downstream, and horses and oxen drowned in such streams as the North Platte (which nowadays hardly flows at all, due to irrigation and other water withdrawals). Travelers tried to schedule their voyages so they would arrive in the drier season, when river and stream levels were at their lowest, although the risks were still high. In such abundance, water was viewed as an enemy.

During the 1800s, we had little knowledge of how to conquer our watery foes. The attempts to retain river or stream waters often resulted in flooding. Dams overtopped or collapsed, sending torrents of water downstream, or at least resulting in water going where it wasn't intended. When a dam leaked — a sure sign that complete failure was imminent — patching was often done with straw and mud. Those faulty dams were highly dangerous. In one instance, the Johnstown Flood of 1889,[3] the collapse of a dam in Pennsylvania resulted in the deaths of 2,210 people and the destruction of 1,600 homes. This truly frightening disaster was the most significant in terms of the loss of life and property, but such floods were relatively common in the 1800s.

Even as late as 1928, we had more water than we could control; when Southern California's St. Francis Dam collapsed, it released a 15-billion-gallon flood

that was one of the greatest civil disasters in American history. The water began as a seventy-five-foot-high wave and scoured a path to the sea two miles wide and seventy miles long. In its wake it left much of Ventura County under yards of muck. The final death toll was nearly five hundred; weeks later, bodies continued to wash up on beaches as far away as San Diego. A horrified journalist wrote of the flood's aftermath: "Thousands of people and automobiles are slushing through the debris looking for the dead. Bodies have been washed into the isolated canyons. I saw one alive stuck in the mud to his neck."[4]

Going from too much to too little didn't happen overnight. The change from wet to dry has been incremental and has as many causes as there are people. And, in fact, people are one of the causes of our water crisis. We have more than doubled our population during the past sixty years: in 1950, the U.S. population was about 150 million; in 2006, we reached

300 million.[5] And our growth rate isn't showing any signs of slowing. It doesn't take a genius to realize that twice as many people need twice as much water.

Another cause for the shortages we're seeing is that, as a nation, we've also been profligate with water usage. As individuals, we water lawns and flower gardens, take long showers, use water-inefficient dishwashers, and eat excessively water-dependent foods, such as grapes, tomatoes, and cantaloupe. With more people, we each need to use less. The slogan "Live simply, that others may simply live" is quite applicable to water usage. A related problem has been the unprecedented urban population explosion in areas that receive little rain. Such dry cities constantly struggle to provide water for thirsty residents, yet at the same time their government officials do their best to entice industries that use millions of gallons of water.

In 1993, in California alone, food-processing plants used 12 billion gallons of water annually; this was reported by the food industry itself in response to a survey.[6] More up-to-date numbers are not available, according to the U.S. Department of Agriculture (USDA). Rather than grow crops only in the areas of the country where they can be naturally sustained with rainfall, we've become reliant on irrigated agriculture, which is a tremendous user of a now-scarce resource. In addition, the trend toward larger and larger dairy facilities, hog factories, and massive flocks of turkeys and chickens have in turn led to "cones of depression" (wherein local water sources are depleted) and to the pollution of surface water and groundwater. The dairy industry, in particular, is culpable of both depleting and polluting.[7] In this book, we'll look at how the wells are running dry in high, arid areas and what that means for the water-dependent crops that feed and clothe our nation and put meat and milk on the table.

There are no easy answers to any of these challenges. It took more than a hundred years to deplete our water resources, and even if we take immediate measures, it is likely to take an equally long time to replenish our water supply. Still, we must begin to understand the crisis at hand and take concrete steps individually, regionally, and nationally in order to prevent the full-blown catastrophe we're headed toward.

Today's State of Emergency

When Boutros Boutros-Ghali was departing from his position as secretary general of the United Nations in 1996, he predicted that in the near future, wars would be fought over water, not oil. While he may not have had the United States in mind specifically, the struggles for water here and in other industrialized nations are becoming acute. Very quickly, the United States has become a country that is desperately seeking new sources of water. Although our federal administration's current attention is on oil, it won't be long until our nation will be forced to shift our focus to finding or conserving more water. Given our aggressive approach to our oil shortage, it's easy to imagine that, if the water crisis is left unchecked, we will become equally aggressive in diverting water from sources north and south of our borders.

The water problems we're facing today are multifaceted and regional, but they must be understood as a whole and addressed as a national issue. In this book, we'll cover the long and bitter negotiations among western states that have led to an overallocation of the waters of the Colorado and Rio Grande, and how that will soon lead to shortages of water in major southwestern cities and their surrounding water-dependent farms and ranches.

No area of this country is safe from the impending water crisis, as you will see in this book: water wars have broken out even in well-watered Florida, New York, and the Midwest;

irrigation wells are running dry across the country, threatening our food supplies; and global warming adds more uncertainties. We'll look at the various technological solutions to the water shortage that have been proposed — from removing salt from seawater to towing glaciers from the polar regions — and evaluate their feasibility.

In just a few short decades, we have depleted our water supply. In the eastern states, which once had an abundance of water, bitter disputes and legal battles have become commonplace over water shortages caused by overappropriation. In the western states, where water has always been in short supply, population growth in dry areas has led to water shortages that threaten to severely restrict or perhaps even bar further growth. It could well be that burgeoning western cities such as Las Vegas, Phoenix, Albuquerque, San Diego, and even Los Angeles and San Francisco may begin to experience population declines when what is now a search for new sources of water becomes an absolute lack. And predicted shortages of water in California's Central Valley, combined with the current water depletion in the High Plains, could bring to a halt the productivity in two of the most productive agricultural areas in the United States.

We've arrived at this state of severe shortage because we've excessively interfered with nature's hydrologic cycle. Left undisturbed, water is fueled by the sun and gravity to continuously move through a succession of phases that leave us with an ongoing water supply. The sun's energy evaporates seawater from the oceans' surface, leaving behind the salts and circulating the water into the atmosphere. After wind currents carry the moisture-laden air over land, the increase in relative humidity eventually causes the water to condense and produces precipitation, in the form of rain, fog, snow, and the like. When the water falls to earth, some of it immediately evaporates into the sky, another portion runs off the land to creeks, streams, and rivers, and some infiltrates the ground, in a process known as *recharge*. A portion of that groundwater near rivers and streams eventually emerges from the ground, in a process called *discharge*, to augment the surface flows of rivers or streams.

When we pump groundwater, as we've done excessively over the past decades, it essentially interrupts this cycle by removing water that would have otherwise been discharged from aquifers to rivers, streams, and other surface water bodies. We've also interfered with this cycle by diverting water from its normal path of renewal and have instead used it in ways and places that nature never intended. Transferring water from the Colorado River and irrigating desert soils (so that water never returns to the Colorado) is interrupting the cycle. In addition to overuse, we have fouled our water supply with salts, heavy metals, antibiotics, and bacteria, and we have stored it in giant reservoirs. While evaporation is a problem in these reservoirs, not nearly as much evaporates as would in the ocean, nor does this evaporation result in rain clouds that ensure the transportation of water from sea to land. This interference has caught up with us, and we are paying the penalty in many ways: water shortages, food shortages, depleted aquifers, and dehydration.

No new water is being or will be created — all we will ever have is what there is now. So *Not a Drop to Drink* examines in detail the myriad dilemmas facing our country's water supply, with an eye to how we got here and what we can and must do to ensure a healthy water and food supply for our children and grandchildren. There *are* many things that can be done to alleviate America's water shortage. Each chapter of this book focuses on a different set of problems and offers solutions. Ultimately, the success of each solution relies on all of us. While it may seem daunting to think about taking on such a widespread and dire problem, big problems can be solved when we act together.

No matter the language, no matter the culture, no matter the society, it is universally recognized that water equals life.[8] With the knowledge and suggestions in this book, I urge you to take an informed stand for life — and for the precious little water we have left to sustain it.

one

TAKING WHAT IS
NOT THERE

Promises of Hypothetical
Water in the West

The Fight over the Colorado River

The Colorado River originates from the melting snowpack on the western slopes of the central Rockies, and for more than 1,400 miles it continues to flow, mostly through lands of little rain.[1] Towering bluffs surround the river's passage, retaining it in a deep canyon that in some places is as much as 5,000 feet below the surrounding tablelands. In the millennia of its existence, the Colorado River has carved immense canyons into the rocks in its path. Cataract Canyon, Marble Canyon, and the Grand Canyon are some of the most magnificent examples of the power of water and sediment grinding down solid rock.

From its brawling emergence near Granby, Colorado, until it becomes lost in the sands near the Gulf of Mexico, the Colorado River gives true meaning to the adage "Whiskey is for drinking; water is for fighting." The river has been dammed many times and has inspired more battles than any other river in this country. It is the subject of such controversy because it has what the West is so sorely lacking: *water*.

The Colorado River didn't used to peter out in the sands of its delta, just south of Yuma, Arizona. Aldo Leopold, the famed naturalist and conservationist, visited the Colorado River delta in the 1920s, describing it as a rich, verdant area, filled with flora and fauna.[2] At that time, there was no central branch of the Colorado — rather, the waters parted into many rivulets, all entering the Gulf of California and, in the course of passage, creating massive wetlands. No longer. Recent estimates indicate that only 10 percent of the flows in the 1920s now reach the gulf, and this trivial amount is heavily polluted with agricultural runoff — pesticides, herbicides, and fertilizer.[3] What was once a water-filled paradise is now mostly a mud flat. It is a sign of the desperation in this situation that Mexican and U.S. environmental and conservation groups are applauding the addition of untreated wastewater and other heavily polluted flows to bolster the once-flourishing wetlands.[4]

As various entities plan to return fouled water to the river, and other groups are advocating these efforts, the freshwater in the Colorado has been the point of contention between the cities of Phoenix and Las Vegas (more on this in chapter 4). The water from the Colorado is also ending up in places where until recently it was never found: as drinking water for Los Angeles, San Bernardino, and San Diego, and as irrigation for citrus and date groves in California's Imperial Valley and alfalfa and cotton fields in San Diego County. A massive aqueduct transports this water from the Colorado River to points west. Urban folks in Los Angeles and San Diego claim that farmers in the Imperial Valley are engaged in wasting water. Farmers respond that without irrigation water, food would become short in the burgeoning coastal cities.[5] Ultimately, the secretary of the interior will referee this battle and decide who is to receive this out-of-basin diversion. If the water is taken from agriculture and directed to the cities, farmers in the Imperial Valley will lose, and if the water continues to flow to the farmers, there won't be enough water to supply the area's huge urban populations. The sad fact is that there is not enough to satisfy the thirsty residents of the coastal cities and to irrigate crops in the Imperial Valley.

Upstream from the aqueduct that transports water to the Imperial Valley and to Los Angeles is Reservoir Powell, behind Glen Canyon Dam, the newest on the Colorado River. This gigantic reservoir — sprawling across southern Utah and northern Arizona — reached its optimal level in 1980;[6] it had by then already inspired a fierce controversy, one that continues to this day and shows no sign of abating. One side, the Friends of Lake Powell and their allies, insists that Reservoir Powell is beneficial and serves the purposes for which it was built — to store water, control flooding, provide recreation, generate power, supply drinking water, and trap sediment.[7] The other side, led by the Glen Canyon Institute, claims that damming Glen Canyon to form Reservoir Powell was a travesty and that the reservoir is barely contributing to the highly questionable purposes for which it was built. The Glen Canyon Institute believes that the Southwest could get along without the small amount of electricity generated and without the even smaller amounts of drinking and irrigation water provided,[8] and its members are calling for the Colorado River to be restored in the canyon. They also point out that the reservoir's water is subjected to evapotranspiration by exposure to sunlight in the hot, dry area. If Reservoir Powell and the Glen Canyon Dam were removed, they assert, the United States could honor its commitments to the country of Mexico and allow the once-verdant delta region to return to its former glory.

But as this battle continues, the water in Reservoir Powell has shrunk in volume due to a drought, and water releases have continued unabated to satisfy contractual obligations made with downstream states.[9] The reservoir reached its lowest level in April 2004, when it was 149 feet below "normal." Hite Marina, on the upper reservoir, was landlocked at least 1 mile from the new shore of Reservoir Powell. Several other marinas were unusable, and one perched on top of what had become a cliff.[10] Many features — such as the Cathedral in the Desert and the Moki Fort — were above the water line and exposed for the first time since Reservoir Powell had filled behind Glen Canyon Dam. Archaeologists scrambled to identify sites used by indigenous peoples (the Anasazi, now apparently the Pueblo dwellers in the Rio Grande Valley) that had been inundated when the reservoir filled.

Since then, precipitation in the southern Rockies, which feeds the Colorado and its major tributaries, has returned to normal or even above normal. The impoundment, while still low, will likely rise as snowmelt in the Rockies will result in more water coming into Reservoir Powell than is released. But climatologists say that Reservoir Powell will not return to its "normal" level of 3,700 feet above the sea unless there is above-average precipitation (as well as runoff) for five years.[11] Some western hydrologists believe that the reservoir will never return to normal, leaving the proposed pipeline to St. George high and dry and calling into question the feasibility of satisfying the Colorado River Compact. (Reservoir Powell was built to provide a steady source of water to meet the Compact's requirements.) If they're right, the small towns dependent on drinking water from the reservoir will be forced to look elsewhere. The Glen Canyon Institute is quietly exultant, asserting that Mother Nature (in the form of a drought) is doing what fearful politicians would not.

The Glen Canyon Institute states that Reservoir Mead can meet all the purposes for which Reservoir Powell was built.[12] The Friends of Lake Powell assert, by contrast, that the giant reservoir in the desert is bringing great prosperity to the formerly impoverished region.[13] Houseboat and pleasure boat rentals pump millions of dollars into the local economy. Fishermen and tourists come from many miles away to enjoy the quiet backwaters and spectacular scenery of Reservoir Powell. Highways that lead to launching areas and marinas are filled each Friday and Sunday afternoon with cars and SUVs towing fishing boats, ski boats, pontoon boats, and all other types of pleasure and personal watercraft. Reservoir Powell has indeed become a destination for folks from Denver, Salt Lake City, Phoenix, and even such far-flung places as Kansas City and Los Angeles.

In addition to praising all these dollars from anglers and pleasure boaters, the Friends of Lake Powell also tout the cheap electricity produced by Reservoir Powell's hydropower turbines and the availability to the Navajo Nation of water for drinking and irrigation. They point to the accessibility afforded to a formerly barren and inhospitable region. The number of annual visitors to Glen Canyon, only a few hundred prior to the closing of Glen Canyon Dam, has soared to two million.[14]

Although the tributaries feeding the Colorado River and Reservoir Powell were flowing at full volume in 2006, there is no surety that precipitation will continue at that rate. Indeed, the record shows that the period on which "normal precipitation" is based may have been an anomaly. There is no doubt that the American West and Southwest are prone to prolonged periods of drought. Some of these periods are relatively short, five years or so. Others have lasted for two centuries or more.[15] Such a long cycle, dry even in the wettest years, was what led John Wesley Powell to tell Congress that the area would never support a large population. The growth of large population centers — Salt Lake City, Albuquerque, Las Vegas, Phoenix, and others — in this area have led to demands for more water than the compact and other agreements (collectively called the Laws of the River) have allocated, and more than the Colorado River is capable of delivering.

For all the fussing and fighting over the water in the reservoirs, sufficient water is not reaching the thirsty populations in the growing cities, nor is the United States honoring its commitments to Mexico. The problem is that the Laws of the River — a hodgepodge of compacts, contracts, and case law regarding the area's water rights — delegates more water than what is available.

The Colorado River Compact was finalized in 1922. It essentially divides the Colorado into two segments — the Upper and Lower basins — with Lee's Ferry, near the northeast tip of the Grand Canyon in Arizona, being the dividing point. The Upper Basin states are Colorado, Utah, and New Mexico. The Lower Basin states are California, Nevada, and Arizona. The Upper and Lower basins are each allowed to take 7.5 million acre-feet

(1 acre-foot is equal to 325,851 gallons) of water from the river per year for "domestic and agriculture" uses.[16] An additional 1.5 million acre-feet are technically supposed to be delivered to Mexico, according to the 1848 Treaty of Guadalupe Hidalgo, but this mandate is generally ignored.[17]

Since 1922, court cases and further agreements between states have complicated this divvying up to the point where some of the rights are now referred to as "paper water" and others as "wet water," which is a way of recognizing that the water rights being determined are partially about water that isn't always available. In wet years, "paper water" becomes wet; in dry years it is "just paper."

When all the water rights are considered and totaled, the volume of water that is spoken for and that may leave the Colorado is 16.5 million acre-feet. An additional 2 million acre-feet is lost each year in evapotranspiration, due to the gigantic reservoirs on the Colorado, bringing the total to 18.5 million acre-feet.[18] But for the past several decades, the Colorado River has flowed at a volume of 15 million acre-feet.

By any calculation, more is appropriated than the Colorado River is capable of delivering. (By the time the river enters Sonora, Mexico, where the Colorado once flowed freely, there's a mere trickle of water that has transformed the area into a sea of giant mud and sand flats.) The result has been ongoing battles over the river's water between the states of the Upper Basin and the Lower Basin, most intense between the cities of Las Vegas and Phoenix. Some criticize the gigantic reservoirs on the Colorado for the loss of 2 million acre-feet per year. Yet without those reservoirs, which store snowmelt for release at a later and slower pace, the Upper Basin could not provide the mandated 7.5 million acre-feet to the Lower Basin, or any of the 1.5 million acre-feet promised to Mexico (some amount is always sent south of the border, mostly to show good faith).

The solution has little to do with whether the water is

used by Las Vegas or Phoenix, or for irrigation or drinking. The water simply isn't there. Fighting over nonexistent water isn't going to make it appear. Any solution must address the actual — rather than the fantastical — amount of water that the Colorado River contains and then apportion that amount on the basis of need.

The Rio Grande Struggles to Meet Increasing Demands

In many ways the Rio Grande resembles the Colorado: both are born of snowmelt in the Rockies, both travel long distances from their headwaters to their mouths, both are the largest rivers in their area, and both are overappropriated to the point of occasionally becoming dry before they empty into their oceans. But the Rio Grande differs from the Colorado in many ways. The main difference is in precipitation: The Colorado — once it leaves the Rockies — flows through the Colorado plateau and a desert; the Rio Grande flows through a land of moderate rainfall. Also, the Colorado is the *only* river in vast areas of the West; the Rio Grande is just one of many rivers (although it is the largest) in its region. And while the Colorado River has been at the core of many disputes, treaties, and compacts as it flows through several states and into another country, the Rio Grande's water rights, while adjudicated in courts of law, have never been disputed with such intensity as the fights over the waters in the Colorado.

The Rio Grande has its headwaters in the southern mountains of Colorado, then flows through New Mexico and Texas, and those states have generally cooperated rather than competed. The Rio Grande Commission, which was formed in 1938 with members from all three states, apportions flows and manages the dams and reservoirs. So, with all this cooperation and lack of conflict, it would seem that the Rio Grande must be flush with enough water for all. Unfortunately, due to various uses and water rights that claim more than the amount of water available, the Rio Grande at Albuquerque barely flows. To fully understand the problem, we need only to follow the river's progression and watch its water levels wildly fluctuate.

Just west of Taos, New Mexico, a bridge on U.S. 64 crosses the Rio Grande. The river is about 800 feet below, and at this point in its 2,000-mile journey to the sea from the snowmelt and springs in Colorado's southern Rockies, it is a mighty and roaring river. From the bridge, the noise of the rapids can be heard, even though the river is so far below that it resembles a trickling blue mountain stream. Occasionally, river runners in kayaks, canoes, or rafts may be spotted — tiny dots on the roaring waters.

The view from the International Bridge between Brownsville, Texas, and Matamoros, Tamaulipas, Mexico, appears to be of a different river. By this point the Rio Grande has traveled through all of New Mexico and the border area between Texas and Mexico. The barely flowing water is a putrid greenish yellow, filled with herbicides, pesticides, and fertilizers carried by the "return flows" from irrigated agricultural lands and with the polluted discharges of the *maquiladoras* (U.S. factories that proliferated after the North American Free Trade Agreement). A few miles downstream, where the Rio Grande once flowed with a rush into the Gulf of Mexico, there is no river. A sandy low area, now easily crossed by foot (causing great problems for the border guards), is all that is left of the mighty Rio Grande.

On its path from its tumultuous birth in the mountainous pine and fir forests north of Durango, Colorado, to its unheralded and silent death in the sandy flats near the Gulf of Mexico, the Rio Grande is repeatedly diverted and polluted. Yet it's impossible to say exactly when and where and how much, because it's unknown how much water is in the river and how much has been appropriated.[19] It would seem elementary that determining how much to take requires a determination of how much is there. Yet the only evidence we have that more water is being taken than is there are several long stretches of dry river bottom.

We need only to follow the Rio Grande the 1,000 or so miles between Albuquerque, New Mexico, and the Brownsville–Matamoros area to see the effects of overappropriation on a river that used to flow freely through that entire region. Just downstream of Albuquerque, the Rio Grande sometimes dries up completely, as that burgeoning city takes all that is left from agricultural irrigation and the pueblos farther upstream. Only the presence of a tiny endangered minnow (the silvery minnow), which spurred a lawsuit by an environmental group, has forced Albuquerque to leave a trickle flowing. Farther downstream, several tributaries add water, and by the time the river reaches the El Paso–Juárez area, the Rio Grande is once again flowing and available for use by those cities. Proceeding downstream, several rivers flowing north from Mexico add waters until the river is impounded in the Lower Rio Grande Valley. From Amistad and Falcon reservoirs on down, the Rio Grande is used to irrigate immense plantations of cotton, sorghum, melons, oranges, grapefruit, and other citrus fruit, and by the time it reaches the Brownsville–Matamoros area, the river is depleted and polluted.

The Rio Grande constitutes a boundary between two sovereign nations, but disputes over water have not been as contentious as those on the Colorado. Recently, the Mexican government, in response to complaints by ranchers in the Lower Rio Grande Valley, fulfilled its commitment and provided flows to the Rio Grande. The Treaty of Guadalupe Hidalgo, signed in 1848, spells out the obligations of the United States and Mexico.[20]

The population on both sides of the border on the Lower Rio Grande is growing, which only points to increasing water needs. The area from McAllen to Brownsville, Texas, on the U.S. side and the corresponding area on the Mexican side, from Reynosa to Matamoros, are rapidly growing and demanding water. In addition, there are many RV and trailer home parks in the Lower Rio Grande Valley to which folks from colder climes flock in winter (they're known as "snowbirds"), swelling the populations and creating even more demand for water. There is also a burgeoning agricultural industry — cotton, grain sorghum, and citrus are all heavily dependent on irrigation — in the Lower Rio Grande Valley (which, that far downstream, is actually the Rio Grande Delta). All these demands have led to "taking more than what is there" and, consequently, the waters of the Rio Grande quite often never reach the sea.

When the waters do flow into the Gulf of Mexico, the cities, the irrigators, and the residents who rely on the Rio Grande for vital needs claim that the uncaptured and unused water is "wasted." About 20 billion gallons — about 61,249 acre-feet — of water enter the gulf in wet years. This is a mere trickle compared to the days when the Rio Grande ran wild and free. The Lower Rio Grande Valley is a shadow of its former self. Even the Sabal Palms Refuge of the Audubon Society is suffering the ills of a declining water level: the namesake palms are dying along with the birds and mammals that live there. The U.S. Border Patrol has a difficult time patrolling a dry river bed — where illegal immigrants once had to swim, they now can walk. Brownsville is well upstream from the Gulf of Mexico, but it is an international seaport. The existence of that seaport is now dependent on a channel that was dug from the ocean. Once the home of jaguars, parrots, and other species in this watery world, the area is desolate and has been forsaken by former inhabitants.

To respond to the needs for potable water of the growing population on the Lower Rio Grande, the Brownsville Public Utilities Board has proposed constructing a weir or dam to "store the waters of the Rio Grande" so that there is a constant drinking-water source. The impoundment created by the dam will flood a portion of Sabal Palm Forest Wildlife Community of the Lower Rio Grande National Wildlife Refuge. Sabal palms once grew profusely along the edge of the Rio Grande in small stands or groves extending about 80 miles upstream from the Gulf of Mexico. Today, only a small portion of that forest remains, protected on 527 acres of the National Wildlife Refuge and on the Audubon sanctuary. For that reason, among others, the dam is opposed by environmental and conservation groups in the Lower Rio Grande Valley.

This proposal has gone back and forth for at least three decades. In 1999, for example, the Brownsville Public Utilities Board claimed that the project was "close to reality"[21] and all that was lacking was state and federal funding. That funding has not been forthcoming, and the project still has not begun. While the dam was originally designed to serve the water needs of a number of communities in the Lower Rio Grande Valley (Port Isabel, Allen, Harlingen, and Mission, to name but a few), the current proposal is only for Brownsville,[22] in recognition that the Rio Grande no longer contains sufficient water to meet the needs of all the communities.

In addition to the lack of water, the weir, or dam, itself has become the subject of controversy, and state and federal governmental agencies may not even provide funding because of the issues raised by members of the local Sierra Club group and their counterparts in Mexico. The importance of allowing the Rio Grande to flow downstream to Brownsville and Matamoros, in order to alleviate the problems with the ecosystem, is also becoming more widely recognized. Jaguars and other species dependent on a forested floodplain have been harmed by the overappropriation of water — and will be driven to extirpation by further withdrawals. If, on the other hand, the riparian zone returns, it is likely that forest- and water-dependent species will once again flourish.

[WHAT YOU CAN DO]

Citizens across this country must become involved in the water struggles in the Colorado and Rio Grande rivers. Up until now, water appropriations and water rights have been left primarily in the inconsistent hands of politicians, with an occasional intervention by local, state, and federal courts. The results have been a hodgepodge of self-serving agreements and decisions, with much more water being awarded than is there. Both the Colorado and the Rio Grande occasionally fail to reach their respective seas, leaving those downstream literally high and dry. Ecosystems that developed in wet times over millions of years have been extinguished. Politicians of all stripes are interested in protecting the interests of their constituents and especially influential constituents. Courts interpret the laws drafted by these politicians — and in the absence of laws, issue Solomon-like decisions, ultimately benefiting no one.

The appropriations, treaties, compacts, and agreements relating to the fate of the waters of the Colorado and Rio Grande have been negotiated, for the most part, behind closed doors. Even when the doors were open, the discussions often turned to arcane and complex matters beyond the ability of ordinary citizens to comprehend. But, as has been long noted by the plumbing community: "There ain't nothing mysterious about it, water flows downhill." To which is added by westerners,

"Or toward money." Too often, wealthy ranchers and farmers, industrialists, and developers of ski resorts, golf resorts, and gated communities have been allowed to dictate who gets the water and how much. All of this comes at the expense of those less influential and less privileged. But the fact remains that the wealthy and the poor require the same amount of water for drinking. Other uses favor the influential — landscaped grounds, brimming pools, and long, luxurious showers.

Water has been appropriated on the basis of "beneficial use."[23] If it isn't used, it is "lost," and the "use" goes to someone else. Quite often, that someone else has quite a bit of money. There is nothing particularly wrong about this. After all, if the community at large benefits from ranching and agriculture, industrial products, or housing, then water should indeed be appropriated for those uses. But what is lacking in this equation are the costs of using every last drop of water. When this happens, we can't maintain a diverse fishery in the Rio Grande or Colorado. There is a benefit to the Lower Rio Grande inhabitants if a healthy and vibrant flow of water enters the Gulf of Mexico — enough for drinking and other individual uses, as well as irrigating the large citrus fruit plantations — and, correspondingly, there is little long-term benefit to constructing a weir or dam to capture the waters for the sole benefit of the citizens of Brownsville. There is a benefit to Mexico if the delta region of the Colorado River is green and resplendent with fish and wildlife. The delta suffers considerably if there is no or little water.

While it is certain that politicians will continue to play a major role in determining the ultimate fate of the Rio Grande and Colorado, it is also certain that the first goal of any politician is to get reelected. While rich ranchers, farmers, industrialists, and developers may contribute heavily to the campaign funds of politicians for hire ("I can't be bought, but I can be rented real cheap"[24]), there is still a one-person, one-vote rule in this country, and politicians do what a majority of their constituents want.

It is well known along the Rio Grande Valley, from Taos to Brownsville, that water must be conserved and used efficiently. To that end, various conservation programs have been instituted — some voluntary, some mandatory. A few conservation steps, if practiced by many, can have dramatic results. Every resident should check for leaks, buy water-efficient appliances, and recycle water at every opportunity. Many citizens now use gray water (from dishwashing, cooking, doing laundry, and bathing) to nourish plants, gardens, and lawns.[25] Others have switched from grassy lawns to dyed gravel, showcasing plants that require little or no water, such as species of cactus. Water departments in cities and towns in the Rio Grande Valley believe that the most wasteful use of residential water is in landscaping, and if steps are taken to convert from water-dependent grounds to those more suited to an arid climate, water usage would be greatly reduced.[26]

In addition to personal conservation steps taken by those directly dependent on water from these vital waterways, citizens everywhere must inform their elected officials that the waters of the Rio Grande and Colorado are important to everyone. The residents of Brownsville or Harlingen are not the only ones who are affected: the Lower Rio Grande Valley is important to this entire country — for recreation, tourism, and agriculture. Such matters should not be left to the greased palms and self-serving decisions of officials in the basins of the rivers. What happens in the basins of the Rio Grande and Colorado is just as significant to New Yorkers as to Arizonans, since, in addition to affecting the food supply, the fate of those rivers will dictate the fate of others — such as the St. Lawrence, which provides water to people in New Hampshire, Vermont, Maine, and at least two Canadian provinces. More immediately, if the Lower Rio Grande becomes uninhabitable and inhospitable, hundreds of thousands of residents will be forced to live elsewhere, and all those snowbirds from the Upper Midwest will be looking for other places to spend the winter.

Only with the active involvement of concerned citizens will the waters of the Rio Grande and Colorado once again reach the seas, the verdant delta areas return to their former richness, and citizens be assured of water for drinking and bathing. Several national organizations are involved with assuring that water appropriations are based on reality (the Sierra Club, the Natural Resources Defense Council, and the National Wildlife Federation), but local politicians tend to listen to their constituents rather than national environmental and conservation organizations. It is critical, therefore, that citizens in cities, towns, and villages along the Colorado and Rio Grande rivers become involved. Only that involvement will assure that no more is taken than is there.

two

THE WELLS RUN DRY

The Time Is Up in the High Plains

The "Buffalo Commons"

Deborah Popper, a land-use planner and geographer at Rutgers University in New Jersey, was at her normal task in 1987, reviewing urban and rural population movements.[1] As she perused a large area west of the Mississippi and east of the Rockies, she was struck by the red colors on her computer map. Red denoted population decline, and further investigation revealed that all the red represented a wave of farmers who were leaving due to the costs of sinking ever deeper wells to irrigate their crops. While many of the counties were in the western reaches of the Dakotas (never highly populated to begin with, and where declines might be anticipated), Deborah and her husband, Frank, also noted that there were substantial declines in what they tagged as the "southern Great Plains."

They dutifully reported their findings in a professional journal, inadvertently touching off a firestorm. The reason: rather than simply reporting the numbers, they also suggested a radical solution. Since the area suffered increasingly insufficient water to support agriculture and those engaged in it, why not return the vast, flat, high, and arid Great Plains to a "Buffalo Commons." The Poppers envisioned returning the rural areas of the High Plains to an area where once again the buffalo would roam. The High Plains refers to an area underlain by the Ogallala Aquifer and is a subset of the Great Plains, although the two terms are often used interchangeably. As they saw it, the cultivation of nonindigenous plants (corn, soybeans, cotton, alfalfa, all of which required much water) had wiped out what was once there. Instead of prairie grasses and the animals that depended upon them — the buffalo, prairie dogs, hawks, owls, coyotes, and wolves — an enormous area of the High Plains had been converted to mile after mile of row crops. They foresaw the day when those row crops would wilt and wither from a lack of water. The job of those in the High Plains, they grandly claimed, was to restore the area to what it had been.

What the Poppers, in all their idealism, did not anticipate was that the longtime plains dwellers were not going to just accept that the water supply was waning and thus that their entire way of life should be abandoned. When the Poppers, who had no experience in public speaking, came to present their findings and ideas in town meetings in such spots as McCook, Nebraska, and Oklahoma City, they were greeted with open hostility. As Deborah Popper put it, "Never did I expect to speak to a crowd that was kept under control by uniformed officers."

The Poppers were roundly jeered wherever they appeared. The common criticism was that they were urban easterners who simply did not understand the hardiness of the inhabitants. The most vitriolic attacks came from those who'd never even reviewed the Poppers' findings. Politicians, with fingers to the wind, sensed that opposition would play well with their constituents, so they released statements ridiculing the idea of the Buffalo Commons. The governor of Kansas, Mike Hayden, said the Poppers' idea "made about as much sense as suggesting we seal off our declining urban areas and preserve them as a museum of twentieth-century architecture."[2]

The Buffalo Commons proposal was disregarded largely because it was viewed as an imposition: easterners coming out to the hardscrabble lands to tell farmers and ranchers that what was really needed was for them to get out of the way and let the buffalo roam. The Poppers' prediction that massive swaths of land would be abandoned as the water for irrigation became unobtainable was simply discounted as more foolishness. At that time, water from the Ogallala aquifer, the primary water source for the area, still flowed freely. It was difficult to imagine that this underground water source would not last forever, even if accessing it meant digging deeper and deeper wells with larger and more expensive pumps. And so life continued, without heed for their predictions, as if the wells would never run dry.

The Ogallala Aquifer Dries Out

In the late 1990s, the predictions of the Poppers were harshly realized. In far western Curry County, New Mexico, rancher Edward Jones got up with the sun, as usual. He stretched, then sat on the edge of his bed for a few moments, listening for the chirping of birds. It was eerily quiet. Finally, he went to the kitchen and turned on his faucet to make coffee. The faucet gurgled a few times before spewing a murky mixture of half sand and half water and then finally just air. "What the hell is going on?" Rancher Jones wondered aloud. He turned the faucet off and then tried again with the same results. He strained the murky water through a coffee filter and, muttering to himself, made his morning brew. It tasted of salt and clay.

Later, checking on the center-pivot irrigation system that watered his alfalfa hay field, he discovered that the pumps were clogged with sand and mud. No water was flowing to his bright green plants. Within hours, they were wilting in the full light of the New Mexico morning. The ranch was dry.

The following year, Rancher Jones was forced to switch from growing water-dependent legumes to dryland wheat. The value of his lands plummeted, and along with it the equity on which he had obtained a bank loan in the form of a mortgage. The bank, realizing this, called on Jones for payment of the loan and now owns his land. The rancher is hoping to move in with his son's family in Phoenix, at least until he can find some sort of work in that city.[3]

What happened to Rancher Jones was predicted by the Poppers. In addition, Jones had had warning signs, and he admits to having known that, sooner or later, the water under his property would disappear. The western portion of Curry County is on the shallow fringes of the Ogallala Aquifer, and he was in the danger zone.

The Ogallala Aquifer, also sometimes called the High Plains Aquifer, is a vast underground water storage area (174,000 square miles) extending under most of Nebraska, the western half of Kansas, eastern New Mexico, eastern Colorado, and the Oklahoma and Texas panhandles. It is not an underground sea, but rather an area of rocks, mud, rubble, and sands saturated with water. The Ogallala ranges from a few feet to a few hundred feet in thickness, and it lies anywhere from a hundred feet to several hundred feet below the surface. The depth below the surface depends on the surface topography. In the eastern areas shallow wells (about 200 feet deep) tap into the aquifer; in the High Plains of the western portions, where the altitudes are a couple thousand feet or more above sea level, it takes much deeper wells, and much more powerful pumps, to extract this water.[4]

The Ogallala Aquifer was formed from the erosion of the Rocky Mountains, as snowmelt from the Rockies saturated a vast quantity of rocks, mud, sand, clay, and other erosional debris. Through a variety of geological processes that occurred over a thousand years ago, the entire Ogallala Aquifer became isolated from its source and now receives no recharge from the Rocky Mountains. Some hydrogeologists believe there may be some small amounts of water that return to the aquifer from playas, streams, and other localized storm-water runoff. But even by the most optimistic estimates, the recharge is only 0.5 to 3 inches per year. It is safe to assume that more is taken out than is replaced.

Given that nearly one-third of the water used for agricultural irrigation in the United States comes from the Ogallala, its depletion is a critical issue. Even if conservation measures are mandated and strictly enforced on irrigation, the store of water in the Ogallala is rapidly declining. Recharge, when and if it occurs, is primarily through precipitation, which averages a scant 12 inches per year in the High Plains. The state geologist for New Mexico, for example, has informed the City of Clovis, in eastern Curry County, that at the current rate of use, the Ogallala in that area will essentially be gone by 2010.[5]

In Kansas, which is over the thicker and deeper end of the aquifer, the state geological survey has predicted that if current rates of usage continue, that segment of the aquifer will be completely dry in a hundred years, even in those areas where the saturated layer is more than 300 feet thick. The more critical areas in that state — where irrigation use is heavy and the saturated layer is not so thick — have at most forty years.

While differences in the thickness of the aquifer account for the differences in the remaining years it can be pumped, one thing is certain: whether now or in the lifetimes of our children and grandchildren, the Ogallala Aquifer will be gone if current use continues, and thousands of ranchers and farmers in the High Plains will experience the same fate as Rancher Jones. While wheat, fescue hay, and other less water-dependent crops will continue to be grown (with lesser outputs) in the arid High Plains, the dependence on corn, soybeans, alfalfa, and cotton will end.

What is happening to the Ogallala is also occurring to the remainder of the nation's aquifers, and chapter 3 discusses what is likely to be the result. The Edwards Aquifer in central Texas, the Equus Beds in eastern Kansas, and the Central Valley Aquifer in the rich lands of California are all being depleted.[6] For a sense of the big picture, here is a complete list of water-supply aquifers in decline:

- Basin and Range basin-fill aquifers (southwestern U.S.)
- Rio Grande aquifer system
- California Coastal Basin aquifers
- Central Valley aquifer system (California)
- Pacific Northwest basin-fill aquifers
- Puget Sound aquifer system
- Willamette Lowland basin-fill aquifers
- Columbia Plateau basin-fill aquifers
- Snake River Plain basin-fill aquifers
- Northern Rocky Mountains Intermontane Basins aquifer system
- Sand and gravel aquifers of alluvial and glacial origin
- Pecos River Basin alluvial aquifer (Texas and New Mexico)
- Mississippi River Valley alluvial aquifer
- Seymour Aquifer (Texas)
- Surficial aquifer system (eastern U.S.)
- Unconsolidated-deposit aquifers (Alaska)
- South Coast Aquifer (Puerto Rico)

It should be noted that the aquifers above provide groundwater from Mexico to Alaska and everywhere in between. In some cases (such as the Central Valley of California), steps are being taken to ensure that the water is used sparingly. In other situations, the attitude is similar to that in the area underlain by the Ogallala: "Take it before someone else does."

Seeking Alternative Water Sources

As the Ogallala rapidly dwindles, many have begun looking to other water sources in the region. The Arkansas and the North and South Platte rivers originate in the lofty snow-covered Rocky Mountains, and until about fifty years ago, they had perpetual flows with high spring and early summer levels. But there are not perpetual flows anymore, as these rivers have been tapped out, and the water level is well below the river level. If there is a flow in the rivers due to rainfall or snowmelt, some of that water goes into the Ogallala through openings that once were springs.

By the time the Arkansas River reaches the Kansas border, it is essentially dry, thanks to reservoirs and pipelines leading to the cities of Pueblo, Colorado Springs, and Denver. By the time it reaches its namesake state, the Arkansas is once again a true river because of heavier rainfall in the area. But at that point it is of little use to the farmers and ranchers on the High Plains, who produce the majority of our nation's food. Likewise, the North and South Platte rivers are perennially dry upon their confluence in Nebraska. It is now possible to cross the Platte River in central Nebraska without one's toes getting wet.

The other rivers that course through the High Plains originate on those plains. The Republican, Niobrara, Smoky Hill, Cimarron, Canadian, and Red rivers begin as tiny tributaries in somewhat barren highlands. All the rivers and streams in the area have been overappropriated — which means that the waters are claimed by every small town, rancher, and farmer along the way — while they have also lost natural recharges from springs, seeps, and upwellings as the Ogallala Aquifer has been pumped below the level of these rivers. While water can still be found in the riverbeds during the late winter and spring, a deadly combination of drought, overappropriation, and loss of recharge has led to beds of sand and silt through most of the year.[7]

But conservation would prolong the life of the Ogallala indefinitely: if irrigated agriculture ceases and the aquifer provides only drinking water for the residents of the High Plains, then the Ogallala would remain intact, as removal of the water for residential purposes would equal the recharge coming in from playa lakes and other sources (the rivers of the plains). Under this scenario, the Ogallala would not recover its former level, but it would not be further lowered, as the small amount of water (rainwater and snowmelt) entering the Ogallala would be sufficient to meet residential demand. In order for conservation to work, all the states involved would need to take part, because pumping Ogallala water near McCook, Nebraska, eventually lowers the water level in west Kansas. It is sort of like sipping from a milk shake (albeit a very large one): even though the straw is taking the liquid from one spot, the overall level is lowered. This means that it does little or no good for farmers or ranchers in west Kansas to start conservation measures (using low-head sprayers, letting some marginal lands return to native grasses) as long as their neighbors to the north are acting as if there is no tomorrow. The ultimate answer is one that those who use the waters of the Ogallala for irrigation (to maximize crop production or to grow crops not adapted to an arid regime) do not want to hear: in order for the Ogallala to stop declining, withdrawals for irrigation must cease.

Polluting and Wasting What's Left

Depletion is not the only danger facing the Ogallala. Paul and Kerri Elders lived in Curry County just a few miles from Cannon Air Force Base and about an hour's drive from Rancher Jones's former place. These freelance writers moved to New Mexico in 1992, settling on a few acres, thinking they had found a quiet place to pursue their avocation and their dreams.[8]

In 2002, the Elderses' idyllic life was disrupted when one of their neighbors proposed constructing a large dairy with several thousand cows just a mile up the road. This area — the eastern half of Curry County — was in the deeper portion of the Ogallala Aquifer, and water was available. Paul and Kerri didn't much like the idea of living near a large dairy; they figured that the prevailing westerly winds would mean that they'd spend their days smelling cows and fending off flies. While the government began offering tax breaks to the would-be dairy owners, the Elderses organized some of their neighbors and began looking for ways to oppose the project.

Almost immediately, they discovered the dairy would hasten the ongoing depletion of the Ogallala Aquifer, from which they obtained their drinking water. Literally millions of gallons of water a day would be used to wash down cattle. More significant, such a dairy would immediately contribute to the aquifer's already-high nitrate levels, since the dairy was proposing to drain the feces and urine from the thousands of cattle into a nearby playa — a dry lake with direct conduits to the Ogallala Aquifer.

"The elected officials are going to run us out of water — and use our money to do it with," the Elderses lamented. "This is just hydrological suicide! And what are they going to do when the water is no longer there? I'll tell you what will happen: the dairies will pack up and leave. We'll be holding an empty bag and drinking bottled water. To see what we'll look like, just take a drive south of Portales (12 miles south of Clovis, New Mexico). All you'll see is brown grass and sandy dirt. That is what we have to look forward to."

Actually, when the water runs out, Paul and Kerri can live

anywhere there's a phone line to hook up to their computers. They have the means and the equity in their dwelling and lands to go elsewhere, and that is what they plan to do. They're already looking at houses near Ruidoso and Cloudcroft, areas with dairy-unfriendly high altitudes and steep terrain. But an increasing majority of the citizenry of the region is Hispanic. Mostly low-wage employees of the service industry, they, unlike the Elderses, cannot leave for greener or wetter pastures. They must remain in Curry County while the water beneath their feet goes to satisfy the thirst of agribusinesses.

In addition to supporting the dairy that the Elderses fought against, the economic-development crowd in Clovis encouraged a large cheese plant to locate in the area. According to local critics, this plant will use 1.2 million gallons of water per day. This is bad enough in an area where evaporation (60 inches per year) far exceeds precipitation (14 inches per year), but the managers of the Glanbia Cheese plant are calling for the creation of 18 additional water-polluting and water-depleting dairies in the area to produce the milk that will become cheese. The cheese produced will be exported in enormous blocks weighing up to 500 pounds, not exactly designed for sale in local grocery stores.[9]

It is almost unbelievable that, in this dry land, government officials would be supporting an enterprise that will rapidly deplete a water supply that's already been predicted to be gone by 2010. Instead of adopting strict conservation measures, the government is actively promoting short-term economic development as if there is quite literally no environmental tomorrow. And they're using taxpayer's dollars to do it: total public subsidies for the Glanbia Cheese plant come to a staggering $16.9 million from federal, state, county, and city coffers *and* a $250 million bond commitment from the City of Clovis. Add the fact that no property taxes will be collected for thirty years, and the total incentive package offered the cheese plant is worth about $30 million.[10]

The Impact on Our Food Supply

The combination of depletion and pollution has disastrous ramifications for our food supply. The area of the country dependent on the Ogallala is quite literally the nation's bread-basket. The High Plains area underlain by the Ogallala represents one-sixth of the land mass of the nation, and only 1 percent of our population. But the area produces 35 percent of our food, which is for the most part dependent on water. Some crops grown in this area cannot, in fact, be grown at all without added water. Others have much higher yields when irrigated — not to mention the massive beef feedlots and slaughterhouses of western Kansas and the Oklahoma and Texas panhandles, which require more than 1 million acre-feet of water per year (enough to cover the entire island of Manhattan in 70 feet of water).

But rather than address the problem of depletion — which, admittedly, would take a massive cooperative effort — the region's local governments continue to turn a blind eye. Dumas is a High Plains city located in Moore County in the Texas Panhandle that gets its water from the Ogallala Aquifer. The Dumas City Council voted unanimously to provide 5 million gallons of water per day to a new slaughterhouse, even though the city engineer has acknowledged that, as a direct result, Dumas (population 13,000) will run out of water from the Ogallala in less than thirty years.[11] The engineer explained that the aquifer is not being replenished and that even at the current rate of use it would be dry in about a hundred years.

Thirty years is enough time for the region's children to

grow into adults and find themselves without jobs or even skills they can take elsewhere. They may not even have that long. Although hydrologists in Moore County predict that the aquifer will run dry by 2034, most of the ones I spoke to in private conversations admitted that it will be economically impossible to extract water for cattle and crops well before that date.

As mentioned above, the prices we pay for food raised on the High Plains are likely to soar. There will also be a domino effect, since much of the grain grown with Ogallala water goes to feeding the animals we eat. Corn, wheat, oat, and soybeans (along with harmful-to-humans antibiotics, appetite enhancers, and hormones) are ground into meal and fed to the vast majority of our nation's dairy cows, hogs, chickens, and beef cattle. Other farming areas of the country will have to take up the slack to produce the grains currently growing in the nation's breadbasket. The hitch is that the agricultural areas of this country are already fully engaged in crop production. It could well be that as supplies diminish, the price of everything we eat will rise dramatically.

The Future of Life on the Great Plains

The Great Plains (sometimes called the High Plains) were once the domain of the Commanche, Kiowa, Sioux, Apache, and other nomadic tribes. Itinerant cattlemen, buffalo hunters, drovers, card sharks, and land developers slowly replaced them. Those who wished to settle the barren plains — and make them not quite so barren — in turn replaced these inhabitants. Windmills came first, pumping water from a few tens of feet down; some can still be found decaying on the prairie. Then, beginning around 1945, electric or gas-driven pumps were introduced, and these drew water from a hundred to several hundred feet. But, water, akin to the buffalo, akin to the antelope that once roamed the plains, is a finite resource. Nothing lasts forever, and water — sparkling, cold, life-giving — is no different.

Sooner or later if irrigation continues to draw down the Ogallala, the cities, towns, and villages of the High Plains will either be extinguished or be forced to seek other sources of water, which will be no small feat. In an area that receives 10 to 15 inches of annual precipitation, there are few surface sources, and those have been claimed and are zealously guarded by their users, mostly medium-size cities such as Amarillo, Texas. So, just as cowboys displaced the Indians, just as the cowboys in turn were replaced by feedlots and irrigated grain farms, so these feedlots and grain farms are also slated for inevitable extinction.

The human misery will be tremendous — small towns will disappear and most of the 2 million remaining inhabitants will be forced to leave for greener pastures. This slow exodus has been going on since the mid-1980s, as reported at the time by the Poppers; vast portions of west Kansas, west Nebraska, and the Oklahoma and Texas panhandles are becoming deserted.[12] Ranchers and farmers who have toiled, and whose parents and grandparents toiled, to make their lands productive will continue to see the value of those lands plummet. They will see once-fertile fields replaced by short-grass prairie and dust, will see their ability to make a living disappear, will see their bank loans called in, will see farm supply and implement dealers go bankrupt, will see small-town, home-owned banks gobbled up by banking corporations and then closed, will see ghost towns where prosperous communities once existed, and will see their children forced off the land.

Sustainability can be defined as "meeting the needs of the present without compromising the ability of future generations to meet their own needs."[13] Ultimately there is no such thing as sustainable use of the Ogallala Aquifer for irrigation — that use can only be prolonged, not sustained. If irrigation continues, the Ogallala will disappear; only the timing of that disappearance is at issue. As I found during my travels through Oklahoma, the owners of large irrigation pumps and center-pivot low-head spray irrigation systems get downright testy when it is suggested that they are living on borrowed time, and that their systems — on which they depend — are reducing that time. "You just goddamned flat don't know what the hell you're talking about," one of them huffed and puffed, before returning, red-faced, to his fields. Yet every fall, he knows that the water table has dropped and that next year he may have to drill the wells deeper and get a large horsepower pump — or he'll run out of water. He knows it, and he denies the reality of what it means.

Farmers and ranchers have a tendency to be concerned solely about this year's crop and today's weather. Underpaid as they are, ten years down the road is much too distant to think about, and twenty years means nothing. So they keep on keeping on: irrigating corn, wheat, barley, sorghum, soybeans, cotton, and alfalfa, though most of those crops cannot survive without irrigation that will soon be an impossibility. It could well be that restrictions need to be placed upon aquifer water usage, but those restrictions would need to be imposed by state or federal governmental agencies, and the political will to do that has been lacking. So far, conservation measures have been voluntary or have been established due to circumstances (lowered water table, less water). Unless citizens from the area and across the country speak out loud and often, this situation is unlikely to change.

And yet while farmers and ranchers may be in it to the arid end, others have seen the writing on the wall, and the population continues to plummet. Late last year, as I drove through this area, I found once-thriving villages essentially abandoned, with grain elevators, grocery stores, banks, and retail outlets standing empty. As I drove through, I was most disturbed to realize there were no FOR SALE signs in these towns, because no one was buying. But lots of CLOSED or NO LONGER IN BUSINESS signs were posted on entry doors, and even more broken windows, collapsed canopies, and sparrow and pigeon nests occupied deserted rafters.

Some say that as the pumps run dry, the area should return to short-grass prairie and the buffalo. Others think that natural gas, petroleum, and mineral deposits should be extracted. Yet others are investigating so-called dry-land farming, willing to accept significant reductions in yields along with a reduction in costly inputs: "Maybe we won't make as much in terms of gross profits, but we'll get to keep more of what we make." Still others — university types, mostly — predict that the cities of the Plains are set to become "high technology" or communication centers, with computers, the Internet, satellite phones, and other wonders manufactured and used in the plains — none of which take much water. Whatever ends up happening, the dwindling water supply in this area means that today's life in the High Plains is headed for extinction.

Buffalo Commons Reconsidered

Much has changed since the Poppers began discussing their proposal. In some areas there is no water — wells, rivers, and streams are dry. Everywhere, the population decline has accelerated, and its root cause in many regions can be clearly attributed to the depletion of the Ogallala Aquifer and the consequent decline of farming and ranching. The formation of a Buffalo Commons is no longer a proposal but an almost inevitable reality. Former Kansas governor Mike Hayden, once one of the most vociferous critics of the Poppers' findings, now admits, "I was wrong. Not only was I wrong — in many cases, the out-migration rates have exceeded what the Poppers predicted."[14]

Unfortunately, very few are taking the strict conservation measures that will allow for a smooth transition to a new way of life. Rather, the goal seems to be to "use it before it is gone." Such attitudes do not bode well for the future of the High Plains, except for the advocates of the buffalo. Sooner for some, and slightly later for others, the High Plains will return to what it was prior to the pumping of irrigation waters from the Ogallala Aquifer. There will, no doubt, be urban and suburban pockets dependent on technological industries and other non-water-dependent enterprises, but in between these towns and cities, the buffalo will roam, mule deer and antelope will frolic, and dry, short grass, ruffled by the ceaseless wind, will cover the High Plains once again.

[WHAT YOU CAN DO]

Farmers and ranchers in the High Plains can take the following steps to prolong, though not sustain, the Ogallala: use low-head sprinklers and drip irrigation, and switch to crops that need less water. The latter holds the most promise. The crops grown in the area underlain by the Ogallala Aquifer are heavily water dependent: corn, sorghum, soybeans, alfalfa, and cotton. Wheat and other grains may be raised without resorting to irrigation, but a farmer or rancher must also be willing to accept a great reduction in per-acre yields (though they will also incur less expense in trying to drill for water). There are also types of corn and maize that produce without irrigation, but those varieties don't yield nearly as well as varieties grown with a surfeit of water. Ultimately, however, using water for irrigation

— no matter how conservatively — will completely deplete the Ogallala.

As taxpayers, we also have some power to help preserve the water in the Ogallala. It is federal policy to reward farmers for overproducing. Billions of taxpayers' dollars are spent in farm subsidies that result in the depletion of the Ogallala Aquifer.[15] In order to stop this, we must contact our congressional representatives and request that this subsidy cease; our money should not be going to help support the destruction of our limited natural resources simply to support a dying way of life. (The websites for the House and Senate, http://www.house.gov/writerep/ and http://www.senate.gov/general/contact_information/senators_cfm.cfm, have contact information for all members of Congress.)

Finally, we must initiate all the water conservation measures listed above and the ones recommended by water utilities in major western cities. If irrigation ends, and such measures become part of daily life, the Ogallala will remain a valuable resource. If steps are not taken, the future is dire.

three

CROPS DON'T GROW WITHOUT WATER

The Uncertain Future
of American Agriculture

While the number of people tilling the soil for a living has plummeted — from more than 50 percent of the U.S. population in the early 1900s to less than 1 percent today[1] — farmers continue to exert immense political power and influence in our country. This is not only true in mostly rural states like Iowa, but also in heavily urban areas such as Florida and New York. Several agribusiness organizations — the American Farm Bureau Federation, the National Farmers Union, and various commodity groups representing corn, soybean, cotton, and rice growers, among others — see to it that largesse continues to flow to their enterprises. In fact, some legislators view agricultural issues as the iconic "third rail" — because the career of anyone who dares trifle with them will come to a spectacular end.

That's no idle threat for members of Congress who are intent on getting reelected, and the "ag groups" do send money to get them reelected — as long as those representatives and senators have voted in favor of agribusiness. If there is any doubt about the power wielded by agriculture, it is necessary to look no further than the congressional committees. The person who chairs the House Agriculture Committee is counted among the top leadership. Representative John Boehner, of Ohio, as of this writing the House majority leader, was Agricultural Appropriations Subcommittee chair. This committee is given considerable sway over the federal budget. The situation is similar in the U.S. Senate.

We can also get a sense of how powerful agriculture is by considering how much governmental staff and space it is allotted. The U.S. Department of Agriculture (USDA) occupies the Whitten Building, one of the largest and more impressive buildings in Washington. It is named after Alabama legislator Jamie

Whitten, who devoted his years in Washington to agricultural issues and who was an avid advocate of agri-industrial development and chemical pesticides (he took the lead in rebutting Rachel Carson's assertions in *Silent Spring* in his book *We, The Living*). In addition to the Whitten Building, four other significant buildings in and around D.C. are dedicated to serving agriculture (which, remember, employs less than 1 percent of the population). The U.S. Department of the Interior, by contrast, with duties and responsibilities to serve most U.S. citizens (its agencies include the Fish and Wildlife Service, the Bureau of Land Management, and the National Park Service) takes up only one building. And while the total number of USDA employees is difficult to ascertain, it's safe to estimate that in addition to the thousands of USDA employees in the D.C. area, there are hundreds of thousands in offices throughout the United States.

Of course, the reason agriculture has so much power and receives so much attention on Capitol Hill is that we all need food to survive. And from the concrete canyons of New York, Chicago, Dallas–Fort Worth, and Los Angeles to folks in the wide-open spaces, we are all dependent for our food on a diminishing number of farmers, and a perhaps disappearing mode of western agriculture. We have arrived at the point where 100 percent of this country's population is dependent upon 0.07 percent of the population for the very stuff of life. But that stuff is now threatened because we may not have enough water to keep them in business.

This threat has been recognized by the members of Congress, but they are also beginning to recognize that the farm vote is far outweighed by the suburban and urban vote. Donations to reelection campaigns are all to the good in the eyes of hungry congresspeople, but it is votes that send them back to D.C.

Agricultural Woes along the Missouri

In the well-watered plains of the Midwest, the U.S. Army Corps of Engineers constructed massive dams on the Missouri River for flood control, inadvertently creating hundreds of thousands of acres of sandy land. Indian tribes lost hundreds of thousands of acres of reservation lands that were inundated with water from the impoundments behind the dams.[2] The Army Corps of Engineers also went to great lengths in the late 1800s and throughout the 1900s to support commercial navigation along the Missouri. They converted its braided, meandering channels into a swift channelized ditch through the use of wing dams, ripraps, levees, and miles and miles of revetments. This in turn resulted in silt, sediment, and sand settling out to create a rich floodplain where the river once flowed, accreting more than 100,000 acres of new farmland from Rulo, Nebraska, to St. Charles, Missouri.[3] These accreted lands — being sandy — need massive doses of water to be productive — which is taken from an ever-shrinking Missouri River. Sandy soil doesn't retain water but allows it to flow through to bedrock below. To ensure large yields of corn and soybeans (the two main crops in the accreted lands), massive amounts of water, delivered through various types of irrigation systems, must be applied to the thirsty crops and sandy soil. This water does not return to the river but is taken up by the plants or seeps deep beneath the surface.

In the fall of 2004, I visited a farmer who was growing his crops in the Missouri River floodplain. Although I was there for other purposes (his wife is a member of the Missouri Hazardous Waste Commission, and I was there to present information on the toxicity of lead), he wanted to talk about water. "Just look over there, where the sprinklers don't reach. The corn plants are only a couple of feet tall — and there's no corn on the ears, just cobs. It's not worth anything. I'm not even going to try to pick it. This sandy river-bottom dirt just won't hold water — you've got to keep the pumps running and you've got to keep putting on the water."

A few hundred yards away — across the flat cornfield — is a low embankment that serves as an agricultural flood levee. Just on the other side is the Missouri, now a swift-flowing body of water that's held in check by various manipulations contrived by the Army Corps of Engineers to keep the river open for commercial navigation. Commercial navigation peaked in 1976 and has been in decline ever since, but that has not lessened the zeal of the corps to manage the Missouri River for barges. In the fall of 2005, when barges should have been coming downriver with grains harvested in the upper Midwest, there were *no* barges. The barge industry stated it would no longer venture onto the Missouri River: the water levels were too undependable.

In the spring of 2005 I returned to this area to find that the remaining wetland marshes in the Missouri River floodplain were mostly dry, due primarily to a lengthy drought in the northern plains. The previous year's cattails and reeds rustled in the wind. Chances are that there'll be no water for the female frogs to plant their fertilized egg chains, and even if they do, there will probably be no water for the emergent tadpoles. The ebullient spring peepers' ambitious breeding efforts may also come to naught, as this was going to be another dry year.

It was so dry that the Army Corps of Engineers decided to forgo a "spring rise" release in March because the upstream reservoirs were below the level at which such a release was deemed feasible.[4] The spring rise was designed to emulate the natural rising levels of the river as the snows melt and the rains fall in the northern plains — and to trigger a breeding and spawning urge in the federally endangered pallid sturgeon. Inadvertently, this rise also overtops agricultural levees (low berms designed to keep floodwaters off farm fields for three out of four years) and adds rich sediment to the Missouri River bottomlands. The deposit of sediment allows bottomland farmers to forgo the use of fertilizers — at a substantial savings.

"All these politicians, levee district folks, and the farm organizations are all in a dither about this spring rise," the farmer said. "This year, that ain't the problem. Hell's bells, I'd like to see the river come up — maybe even up to the top of that levee yonder. As it is, though, my intake pipes are above the water line. With this sandy soil" — he kicks the ground for emphasis — "I can plant corn and soybean seeds, but they won't even sprout, because I can't get any water to them. Right now, I own about a thousand acres of nothing."

The farmer walked over to the levee. I followed. He pointed upriver.

"See those sandbars. See those wing dikes. You shouldn't be able to see them. This time of year they ought to be covered with about ten feet of water. But they're all exposed. In some places, you could almost walk across the river, except maybe out there in that barge channel — the corps keeps that dug out in case the barges start going. But there ain't no barges. According to the barge companies, they've given up on even trying to make runs upriver.

"Unless that river comes up some — and quite a bit — I'm not going to be making a dime this year. Oh, I can make it — all of this land is bought and paid for. But those ol' boys that have to make mortgage payments to the bank, they're not going to make it. The bank will own the land, and these guys that tried to make it — well, they'll be renting an apartment in town, working at some fast-food joint, getting paid a minimum wage." He kicked again at the dry dirt on the levee and walked off.

The problem that this farmer and others like him are having is that the Army Corps of Engineers' rules have changed because the U.S. Fish and Wildlife Service asserted that the

Big Muddy, by federal law, must be managed to protect and restore endangered species — the least tern, piping plover, and pallid sturgeon. The Master Manual, a federally approved manual that details how the Army Corps of Engineers manages the Missouri River, was subsequently revised, but the new management plan has led to a dearth of water, exacerbated by a prolonged drought in the upper Midwest. Floodplain farmers expect a certain level of water in the river. That level is not there. While there's some truth to the statement that farmers are never happy ("too wet, too dry, too hot, too cold"), those dependent on the Missouri River had come to expect that the corps was their friend. After all, the corps had created the rich lands in the floodplain, the corps had managed the river so that there was a cheap method of transporting fertilizer upriver in the spring and grains downriver in the fall, and the corps had managed the water levels in the river in ways that were mostly beneficial to bottomland farmers. But the Army Corps of Engineers is a federal agency and must follow federal laws and rules. Downstream farmers — led by agribusiness interests — have vociferously protested the new Master Manual, but the engineers' hands are tied.

Even while the corps' efforts initially seemed to help farmers, they also created new environmental and agricultural problems. Before the corps did this massive construction on the Missouri River, there were occasional major floods, when the river reclaimed its floodplains and inundated its entire valley from bluff line to bluff line. But those were exceptions, and farmers along the river took those exceptions into account, reckoning that in one out of every ten years they might not get any crops. At the same time, those floods replenished the floodplain with rich sediment and organic matter; this material, washed in from the Rockies and northern plains, meant that not much had to be spent for fertilizer.

The great flood of 1995 was the final straw for insurers,

who had tired of writing checks every time the water damaged something that their policies covered. They informed bottom-land residents that this was the last time that dwellings, barns, and other possessions (propane tanks, for example) would be covered for losses due to remapping of the floodplain.[5] Emergency management agencies dictated that all structures should be removed from that remapped floodplain. Other federal and state agencies (the USDA, U.S. Fish and Wildlife Service, and Missouri Department of Conservation) bought out severely damaged lands where deep scouring ("blue holes") or heavy deposits of sand had rendered the lands unfit for growing anything except cockleburs. But farming continued and flourished in areas that escaped heavy damage. Fortunately for the farmers, most of the rich bottomlands were not heavily damaged or were recoverable (one method of recovery was to plow in the sand — incorporating the sand dunes into the rich, but already sandy, soil).[6]

Nevertheless, while the flood of 1995 triggered changes that were long overdue, it did little to prepare bottomland farmers for a lack of water. The Missouri River farmer I spoke with was correct in focusing on the corps' plans to withhold water from upstream reservoirs. He asserted that there was little or no attention paid to what might happen if the Army Corps of Engineers didn't release water to simulate a natural spring rise. This is the crux of the problem: no water, no crops. While it could well be that the prolonged drought on the northern plains may have led to a shortage of water anyway, the new Master Manual emphasizes protecting the large reservoirs in Nebraska, the Dakotas, and Montana over providing water to downstream farmers. The Army Corps of Engineers, under pressure from the Fish and Wildlife Service, changed the rules. The old rules, which benefited downstream farmers, no longer exist.

The State of Agriculture in the West

The water shortage problems in the area surrounding the Missouri River are significant, and yet this is occurring in the well-watered Midwest, where average precipitation ranges from 36 to 40 inches per year (although some say these averages were based on a time of plentiful rain in the early twentieth century and that the averages are no longer valid).[7] In other agricultural centers of the country, precipitation isn't as plentiful.

The 100th meridian[8] is an imaginary line that divides the country into a precipitation-heavy eastern portion that needs little irrigation and a dry western portion that's utterly dependent on it — it is the lack of precipitation that receives the most attention. The Missouri River rises in the Rocky Mountains on the west side of the 100th, but the confluence with the Mississippi is on the eastern side of this meridian. The arid area west of this divide is where water is most needed to sustain agriculture, although we have seen that what affects the Missouri River upstream also affects those downstream.

In chapter 2, we looked at the travails of farmers dependent on irrigation waters from the rapidly depleting Ogallala Aquifer. It is a simple fact — accepted by everyone who has studied the Ogallala — that at some time in the future, and for some the future is now, the Ogallala will cease to be. Dryland farming or no farming at all will be done in the High Plains of west Kansas, eastern New Mexico, west Texas, the panhandles of Texas and Oklahoma, and western Nebraska. In some parts of eastern New Mexico, where the Ogallala is shallowest, wells that tapped into the aquifer have stopped producing water, and farmers have made a choice between switching to lesser production from dryland crops or selling out for a few bucks and going elsewhere.

The Ogallala's cautionary tale is being repeated in California's Central Valley, where seasonal runoff from the High Sierra used to result in too much water in the spring and early summer and not nearly enough in late summer and fall. Efforts of the Bureau of Reclamation and the Army Corps of Engineers resulted in dams, impoundments, and various diversions that delivered water from the mountains more evenly throughout the year. Thanks to those efforts, the Central Valley was converted from an area that, in wet times, was plentiful with wildlife into an agricultural area that provides a hungry nation with much of its food. This conversion has devastated the wildlife as well as the landscape. Due to evaporation rates, and previous and current groundwater pumping, some lands in the Central Valley are now topped with a layer of salty crust, rendering the lands infertile and unproductive.[9] If irrigation continues — which it will, given the governmental subsidies that allow agriculturists to buy lots of water quite cheap — it is certain that the extent of infertile and unproductive farmlands will increase. Grapes and pistachios don't do well in salty soils.

The Imperial Valley, by contrast, used to be dry all year: 2 inches of annual rainfall, and no runoff from the adjacent desert mountains. Only when the Army Corps of Engineers began manipulating the Colorado River did the Salton Sea fill, and the waters from that sea made the desert bloom and turned the area into a major agricultural center.

At the same time, coastal cities from the San Francisco Bay Area to San Diego have grown by leaps and bounds, which means that these areas are demanding ever more water. So far, that water has been provided by a series of imaginative schemes and costly systems, which will be illuminated in the next chapter. But, essentially, urban sprawl is taking much of the water that has been used to irrigate the nation's crops.

While there is water for all now, that water, its delivery,

and its quantity are the subject of many disputes between the coastal cities and the rural inland. Since, as the saying goes, "water flows toward money," it is likely that the coastal cities will prevail. When water is no longer available to farmers in the Imperial or Central valleys — or is available only in greatly reduced amounts — it could well be that vast areas of California will revert to desert conditions. No longer will agriculture be the leading money maker in the California economy, and no longer will grapes, pistachios, or almonds from California be available in the local grocery store at low prices. Such produce might not be available at all. But even more crucial is that the Central Valley also produces most of the country's lettuce, tomatoes, cauliflower, broccoli, artichokes, and even such staples as onions and potatoes.

The Impact on Our Food Supply

A lack of water will not only mean that farmers in the Missouri River Valley or the area of the Ogallala Aquifer or the Imperial and Central valleys of California will go belly up, but that the teeming masses will go hungry. In addition to being the major source of produce, the Central Valley is also the somewhat miserable home of dairy cows, chickens, beef cattle, and a growing number of hogs — and so meat, milk, and eggs come from the Central Valley as well.

While some of this could be supplied by other portions of the country, it is simply not possible for the farmers in the South — Alabama, Georgia, Mississippi, Florida — or the well-watered Midwest to produce foods in the variety and quantity now produced on the western plains, in the Southwest, or on the West Coast. If farmers west of the 100th meridian run out of water, everyone will suffer.

Repairing the Federal Agricultural Subsidy System

Much of the irrigation water in the United States is used to support agriculture in places that were formerly arid or under water. The U.S. Army Corps of Engineers and the Bureau of Reclamation have dammed literally all major and most minor rivers in this country. The Bureau of Reclamation has dammed, diverted, canalled, piped, and otherwise transported water from distant places to where it can be put to use. The bureau, whose original mandate was to assist small farmers, now directs its attention to providing cheap and plentiful water to the largest agribusiness companies in the world, some of which are multinational corporations. According to various sources, more than 70 percent of all water in the United States and 60 percent of all the world's freshwater withdrawals are used by agriculture.[10] Large, influential corporations own most of the U.S. farms that benefit from this irrigation.

The amount of money that flows directly to agriculturists is immense. The Farm Bill of 2002 was intended to correct this massive drain on the federal budget, but the U.S. Congress granted "variances" that allowed the subsidies, grants, incentives, and funding to continue unabated. Subsidies alone — funds that pay farmers for raising grains such as rice, wheat, corn and soybeans — amounted to $143 billion in 2005.[11] The grains go into poultry feed as well as hog and cattle feed. Water is heavily subsidized, even though the water provided by various dams and canals constructed by the Bureau of Land Management was supposed to benefit only those with 160 acres or less; agribusinesses found loopholes that quite literally opened the gates to much larger spreads.

The subsidies are not evenly distributed — large landowners, corporations, wealthy individuals, and U.S. Congress members rake off most of the money.[12] The formula is: the more food produced, the greater the subsidies. Not only does this reward overproduction; it also rewards those who need such subsidies the least. According to USDA statistics, $104 billion (72 percent) of the farm subsidies went to the top 10 percent of recipients — some 312,000 large farming operations, cooperatives, partnerships, and corporations that collected, on average, more than $33,000 in subsidies every year (not including direct subsidies for overproduction and the additional grants for setting land aside). All this largesse has given rise to the phrase "farming the government," which refers to farmers who receive large checks from the USDA for their set-asides. This situation has gotten so out of hand that many recipients of federal farm subsidies make as much money from USDA checks as they do from raising crops.

In addition to these direct subsidies, the Army Corps of Engineers and Bureau of Reclamation have created indirect subsidies to farmers in otherwise arid or flood-prone locations through dams constructed for irrigation and flood control. The Central Valley of California was once a vast wasteland,[13] alternating between too much and too little water. Seasonal runoff from the Sierra Nevada in the winter and spring months created wetlands where tule reeds, elk, grizzlies, and migrating waterfowl flourished. When this runoff ceased, the heat of summer and fall converted the area to a place where precipitation was essentially nil. The Bureau of Reclamation "came to the rescue," by building dams and diversions, piping water to thirsty farmlands, and equalizing the water flow. In the course of doing this, the elk, grizzly and waterfowl were forced to go elsewhere. Today there are only a few lonely ducks. In the zeal to make the Central Valley productive, the bureau and the farm organizations took a very short view. As the land becomes salty (and infertile and unproductive), as subsidence from groundwater pumping causes damage to residential and commercial buildings, and as the water supply is being fought over by, and diverted to, distant and growing cities, the Central

Valley has lost its claim to being the most productive agricultural area in the world. If the long view had been taken, chances are that fewer acres would have been put into production, less water would have been needed, and many of the problems above could have been avoided.

Fortunately, it is not too late to correct these errors. There are ways of providing direct and indirect subsidies that are much better for the water supply than the current system. One of the primary problems is that the subsidy system has been captured by agribusinesses. As noted, most of the largesse from direct subsidies goes into corporate coffers; not much is given to farmers engaged in sustainable practices (the USDA estimates that 10 percent of growers receive 78 percent of the farm subsidies).[14] For every ear of corn grown in the Central Valley, that means one less ear in the Ohio Valley, with the former requiring much government water and the latter needing no amount other than what is provided from the sky. The big guys use a huge amount of water in producing their crops. For example, growing rice uses a lot of water. Fields are leveled, a 12-inch or so berm (dirt ridge) is placed around the fields, and then the rice fields are flooded with water. It makes little sense to raise rice in the desert and then to be rewarded for that by millions of dollars in federal subsidies — but that is exactly what happens. Growing rice in the Central Valley of California — a former desert in the summer — brings in literally billions of dollars to rice-growing agribusinesses. The most farm subsidies that were received in the entire state of California went to a company with its headquarters in Sacramento County, in the heart of the Central Valley. That rice-growing company received $143.5 million in taxpayers' money from 1995 to 2004. Subsidies in those same years to large growers of all commodities in Kern County totaled $364 million. In the Central Valley's Colusa County, the top recipient of farm subsidies (and number eleven in California) received $6.5 million for rice operations; the second-highest recipient was also a rice grower and got $5.4 million.[15] There's not a family farmer in the lot of recipients. In fact, one would be hard-pressed to find a family farmer in any county — farming in the Central Valley was long ago taken over by agribusinesses that own thousands of acres, all benefiting from subsidies and cheap water. Those engaged in sustainable agriculture — family farmers — tend to grow crops more suited to their area. In the case of the Central Valley, family farmers didn't even try: it was just too hot and dry.

Experimental farm "stations" dedicated to growing rice more efficiently and productively are operated by universities and funded by the U.S. Department of Agriculture. The USDA also directly owns and operates some of these stations. The chief beneficiaries of this research are rice-growing companies. While the USDA claims that such research benefits consumers, this is unproven. What is proven is that the rice-research facilities obviate the need for rice companies to invest in research and development. The federal government does it for them. Rice is one of the most water-intensive plants around — indeed, for a major portion of its growing season, the plants must stand in water. The sad fact is that the federal government is promoting this water-dependent crop and using taxpayer money to do so.

To this direct handout of federal dollars are added indirect subsidies from the Bureau of Reclamation and the Army Corps of Engineers that allow these same agribusinesses to utilize irrigation water at a fraction of the costs of capture and delivery. If these direct and indirect subsidies should end, it is likely that very little rice would be grown in the Central Valley — and there would be a commensurate lessening of water needed for irrigation. But the USDA and the Bureau of Reclamation provide all sorts of incentives with taxpayer money for the water-guzzling rice growers to keep raising this commodity in the desert. The other rice-growing areas in the United States are in the Mississippi River floodplains of Arkansas and Louisiana and in the area of Texas along that state's Colorado River (not *the* Colorado River). Once again, the federal dollars go mostly to large corporations — the top two largest beneficiaries of farm subsidies are in Stuttgart, Arkansas[16] — but at least there's no indirect subsidy pertaining to the capture and delivery of water. There is plenty of water in the Mississippi River, and it is easily available to rice growers without massive federal assistance. Rather than use taxpayer's dollars to provide water to this crop, the federal government — the USDA — needs to identify areas of the country where water is plentiful without any direct or indirect subsidy.

While there is an unofficial "cheap-food policy" in this county, and the USDA and the schools of agriculture at land-grant colleges and universities have done much to keep the prices low, these entities have used the taxpayers' money to do so. A head of lettuce may not cost consumers very much in the supermarket cooler, but the direct and indirect subsidies that have gone into producing that head of lettuce make it very expensive. The billions of dollars from the federal coffers (filled by everyone who pays taxes) that benefit corporate agribusiness are kept hidden.

No one can say with certainty how much the water delivered to a "farm" in the Central Valley is really worth — but it is much more than the $3.50 per acre-foot (325,851 gallons) charged to growers. Until recently, no one knew how much federal money was flowing to the owners of that same piece of real estate. Thanks to the efforts of the Environmental Working Group, which placed the entire USDA Farm Subsidy database on its website, that information is now instantly available. Money in the form of farm subsidy payments and the delivery of heavily subsidized water keeps food prices down. That cheapness, however, is an illusion. We all pay dearly. Cheap food falls in the same category as a free lunch. There's no such thing.

The Future of American Agriculture

Wendell Berry, the Kentucky farmer and author, said it best: "Eating is an agricultural act."[17]

What is eaten determines what is grown. If products that require a lot of water are not eaten, those products are not sold and will not be grown. So it's imperative that we determine which products are sustainable and which aren't. Here's a list of water-wasting culprits that we need to reduce or eliminate our consumption of to preserve our water supply:

> **Pork.** Although local supplies are often drawn down temporarily (in what is called the "cone of depression" effect),[18] with a few exceptions, raising and slaughtering hogs doesn't take a lot of water, and for the most part, the capture and delivery of that water is paid for by the company that owns the hogs. But — and this is where it gets complicated — those hogs are likely fed with grains that were grown with a lot of cheap water and with subsidies. That cheap water and those subsidies were likely provided by the federal government. Raising hogs, it turns out, requires an enormous amount of water. It's indirect, to be sure, but that water must be taken into account.

> **Beef, poultry, milk, and eggs.** While the immediate needs of water for beef and dairy cows and for chickens (although both these species consume large quantities of water) are not great, feeding the animals, as well as the add-on costs of processing to bring that meat, milk, and

eggs to the supermarket, adds to an enormous demand for water. It is estimated, for example, that 1 pound of beef requires 1,000 pounds of water.

Animal Feed. Animal feeds are mostly composed of corn, soybeans, and other grains (milo, wheat) raised in plenitude in areas where irrigation is provided by declining aquifers.

Rice. While the rice-growing areas of this country are mostly ones where water is not in danger, the USDA is promoting this crop in areas of the country that are already in dire straits. Make sure that any rice consumed comes from lands along the Mississippi River.

Grapes and berries. Grapes and various types of berries (strawberries, blackberries, even blueberries) are grown in California's Central Valley, watered intensively — grapes are mostly water — and sold year-round. If such fruits are grown in naturally well-watered areas, much less "government water" is needed, perhaps none at all. Grapes require a moderate (sometimes called "Mediterranean") climate, but many well-watered areas of the country provide this. The drawback to changing growing areas is that most fruits are seasonal, which means that eating fresh strawberries in Maine in February would not be possible.

Cotton and tobacco. Not mentioned to any great degree in this book are nonfood crops. Cotton will grow without much added water, but it does best in southern states where humidity, heat, and precipitation are highest. Unfortunately, cotton is now king in areas that are quite dry (such as west Texas, New Mexico, and Arizona) and irrigation from aquifers, groundwater, and large reservoirs ensures that crop yields are high. Tobacco use in this country has declined significantly since it has been documented as a carcinogen.[19] Tobacco is grown primarily in the East.

The more one digs, the more it becomes evident that this country's food system depends on plentiful and cheap water. But as the population grows and per-person consumption spirals upward, water will become scarce and expensive. The retail costs of all food will skyrocket. Unless several steps are taken, this country's unofficial "cheap-food policy" is likely to disappear simply because of the shortage of water.

For those living east of the 100th meridian, the best step is to purchase locally produced foods that don't need undue amounts of water to produce. If we don't take steps now, in time we may all be forced to eat lower on the food chain — not from choice but because of the rising costs of products that require cheap and plentiful water (which will soon be unavailable) to be produced affordably.

West of the 100th meridian, certain areas may become uninhabitable. There won't be cheap food in the supermarkets of Las Vegas or Phoenix, as the decreasing water supply makes it impossible for anyone to grow anything in the deserts surrounding those towns. Therein lies the rub. Most metropolitan areas west of the 100th meridian depend on reliable sources of mass-produced, affordable foods. If such foods can no longer be grown locally, they'll need to be brought in from areas that receive copious amounts of rainfall. In the future, those areas will be far distant from West Coast cities — at least 1,000 miles. Lack of water and high transportation costs could very well end our cheap-food policy.

It will be comparatively easy for the citizens of Chicago, Indianapolis, and the cities of the eastern seaboard to acquire food. There are already farmers engaged in supplying local consumers.[20] Their numbers will need to be significantly increased, but the market forces of supply and demand will see to that. As usual, one person's loss is another's gain. Central Valley farmers will likely lose and lose big — maybe even go out of business. Ohio Valley farmers will likely gain and gain big. Whether those Ohio Valley farmers make enough money to pay for their products to be shipped to the West Coast remains to be seen. If their prices rise and consumers in western cities absorb the costs, then farmers in the Midwest will flourish. If price increases result in consumers' buying less, then midwestern farmers will sell closer to home.

It is difficult to predict a pleasant future for the residents west of the 100th meridian. Cheap and plentiful water and, therefore, plentiful food supplies are about to run out in the very near future. In northern California and along the coasts of Oregon and Washington, rainfall is sufficient to support many farms, but whether those farms can produce sufficient food to feed Californians is an open question. No doubt seafood will fill a gap — although there are those who worry that we are depleting the oceans' supply of seafood.[21] The problem is one of too many people in a dry land that cannot support its population. While it is easy to regret "what might have been" and to believe we should have heeded John Wesley Powell's admonition that the lands west of the 100th meridian would never support large populations, that provides little solace for the residents of Denver, Los Angeles, and San Francisco, along with Albuquerque, Las Vegas, and the other towns and cities of the desert Southwest. A few will survive on locally produced foods. Still others will pack up and move to the Midwest and the East in a reversal of what happened during the Dust Bowl of the 1930s. Whatever the case, the future is grim if eating habits don't change and moves are not made to more sustainable and less water-dependent foods.

[WHAT YOU CAN DO]

All of us can help alleviate the water crisis today by taking a few steps:

- Eat lower on the food chain. Our consumption of meat, milk, and eggs will need to be reduced significantly or curtailed completely. The production of milk and eggs uses enormous quantities of water (milk cows, for example, drink a lot of water to produce a lot of milk, and eggs require much water to wash off debris ranging from chicken manure to dirt). Processing meats — beef, pork, chicken, fish — also requires much water. Since slaughterhouses and packing plants are located near large cities, it is best to avoid eating meat simply because of the use of water in processing (not to mention other moral, social, economic, and environmental reasons).

- Purchase foods that are grown closer to home. Farms that engage in organic practices don't necessarily use less water; water is not considered an "inorganic" additive. But it is best to purchase foods, as Wendell Berry says, from someone you know. Indeed, the entire concept of Community Supported Agriculture, or CSA, is for consumers to get to personally know the person(s) who produced their food. Food "with a face on it" is the motto of the participants in the CSA movement. When in doubt, visit the farm — if a lot of additive water, or irrigation, is used, buy elsewhere.

- As mentioned above, some foods simply cannot be grown without lots of water. Avoid foods that are heavily water-dependent, or ensure that those foods are produced in places where natural supplies of water are abundant. Rice is the best example: When grown in southeastern Missouri, the Arkansas Delta, or Louisiana's lowland, rice is the ideal food. But when grown in Texas or California, where natural sources of water are at a premium and other sources (reservoirs, canals, groundwater, or aquifers) are required to supply copious amounts of water, those who produce such rice become "welfare queens" by farming the government. Once again, the advice is to know where the food is produced.

- Become an informed consumer. Wendell Berry's words bear repeating: "Eating is an agricultural act." By eating less-water-dependent foods, or those grown in areas where water is plentiful, we place less stress on an increasing shortage of water. Know where your food comes from, and avoid buying foods produced in places that depend on artificial sources of water (reservoirs, canals, groundwater, or aquifers). For more information on buying locally produced foods, see http://www.nal.usda.gov/afsic/agnic/agnic.htm. This site, maintained by the USDA, provides a list of all known sources. Also, there is much information provided on a sustainable agriculture website: http://www.sustainableagriculture.net/.

This is an issue in which individuals can make a difference. If we take some simple steps and become informed consumers, water shortages can be drastically reduced, perhaps even to the point of nonexistence. Many individuals will have to take action to make a difference, but the future depends on our doing so.

four

WATER WARS

Regional Battles Sweep the Nation

Battles over water are nothing new, but as this essential resource becomes more limited, they are becoming more intense. This chapter will examine in detail the water wars that are breaking out all over the country. In the arid West, which has long been accustomed to water disputes, the battles are heating up about who gets the first (and sometimes only) dip. Now, however, feuds have developed in well-watered areas such as the southeastern and northeastern United States.

From the Pacific Northwest and the Klamath Basin to the Gulf Coast and the Apalachicola River, water and who gets it for what use are at issue. On almost every river, creek, and lake throughout the nation, there are those who assert their needs or wants above those of others. Since this problem is pervasive, it would be impossible to detail every struggle. This chapter will focus on those struggles that affect the greatest numbers of people and those that have generated the most controversy. Keep in mind that for every water war you learn of here, plenty more are taking place in courtrooms or in negotiations behind closed doors.

When the issue is water, there seems to be scant room for compromise and even less interest in the welfare of people in other areas and in the environment itself. When water is over-used or polluted in one place, the tendency is to simply look for another source of water. However, we are running out of "elsewheres." There is simply not enough water to meet every need. Instead, we must begin to reevaluate our needs and our water usage — before all we're fighting over is valueless paper, water rights that represent water that's unusable or simply not in existence.

San Francisco versus the Central Valley

"They say it smells like money. It just smells like cowshit to me," commented Ray Donnell, of Bakersfield, as we drove around the vast agricultural valley in central California.[1] We were west of Modesto, following a series of gravel roads through the rich lands of the Central Valley. The land in this area is made rich from diverted snowmelt and runoff from the Sierra Nevada. The mountain wall rises abruptly to the east of the Central Valley, and through a series of dams, canals, and water diversions, this water quenches the thirst of the nut tree groves, vineyards, and dairies that make this area so productive.

"Which way is the wind coming from?" inquired Ray. "Once you figure that out, and you smell cow manure, look in the direction the wind is coming from and you'll see the dairies."

He was right. We stepped out of the car and determined that the wind was from the southeast. Every time we caught the scent of cow flop, we looked to the southeast and saw the metal roofs of the "loafing sheds" of dairies gleaming in the sun. We came eventually to the Kings River, or what was left of it. In the Sierra Nevada, the Kings River is powerful and gushing.[2] Here, several miles north of Bakersfield, it is a mere trickle. Many straws have been sipping, and others gulping, from the same watercourse, which has diminished its strength. More and more frequently, it dries up completely during the dry season. And the small amount of water it does get from its return flows — the water that isn't absorbed by the soil or used by the feedlots and farmlands and thus flows back into the river — has been heavily polluted by fertilizers, pesticides, and cow manure.

Ray and I pulled our vehicle into a dirt parking area on the north side of the ramshackle bridge and strolled down to the depleted river. Along the banks of the Kings were eucalyptus and tamarisk trees, both nonnative species and both water suckers,[3] taking what is left after agricultural irrigation, drinking water supplies, and dairies and feedlots have gotten their share. These trees, however, merely add to the problem. If there were not so many other uses of the Kings' water, the amount taken by the trees would hardly be noticed.

Of course, those Central Valley dairies taking up and polluting so much water don't consist of a few cows grazing in a peaceful green field with shade trees. These cows never set a hoof in a pasture and never see a shade tree. There are thousands of cows in each commercial dairy.[4] When not being milked in an enormous "parlor," the cows spend hours on concrete under an aluminum shelter — eating grains and hay and drinking water, and excreting an enormous amount of manure and urine. One cow excretes about twenty times as much as one human.[5] Given the many thousands of cows in the Central Valley, it is easy to see how this washed, untreated waste has heavily polluted the Kings, San Joaquin, and Sacramento rivers. And this pollution doesn't even include the pesticide- and fertilizer-laden runoff from all the fields in that area, which increases the problem exponentially.

While the food production in this area is undoubtedly destroying the environment and using vast quantities of water, the corporations that own the lands in the Central Valley (very few individuals are landowners in that area)[6] maintain that because there is a market for their products, their practices cannot and should not be altered. The hungry mouths of the coastal cities need to be appeased. And, of course, there is some truth to this. It is much more efficient to transport milk to San Francisco from Modesto than from Wisconsin. Almond trees and other crops from the region won't grow well elsewhere. And while there are vineyards in moderate climates throughout the United States, none are so productive as those in the Central Valley. Indeed, this lush area, and not the Midwest, is sometimes called the nation's breadbasket — and with good reason. The fertile soils, favorable (warm to hot) climate, and abundance of irrigation have resulted in the most productive agricultural area in the world.

Lately, however, this productivity has been questioned.[7] It takes a great deal of water to make the area productive — water that must come from somewhere else and water that is coveted by others. The agricultural area of the Central Valley is not the only area of California that relies heavily on the runoff from the Sierra. Left untouched, that water follows a winding path of waterways of more than 200 miles to the San Francisco Bay. But as that water is used up and polluted in the Central Valley, it starts a chain reaction of problems that have impinged on everything in the water's path.

The first major waterways to be harmed by the Central Valley's overuse and pollution of water are the Sacramento and the San Joaquin rivers, which both depend on tributary streams originating in the Sierra Nevada. The dams, diversions, and canals that were built to guarantee consistent irrigation to the Central Valley have constricted the flow of both the Sacramento and the San Joaquin. The Sacramento River is a bit less depleted and polluted than the San Joaquin, because it drains the northern (and somewhat less developed) portion of the Central Valley. The San Joaquin flows northward and, from southern Kern County to the bayside Contra Costa County, flows through countryside that is intensively cultivated and irrigated, which pollutes and depletes the water that the Bay Area needs.

The problems continue downstream, where the confluence of the Sacramento and the San Joaquin rivers has formed the California Delta. Because of the depletion of these two rivers, the delta is in serious decline. Pollution and freshwater depletion, which has allowed salt water to flow into places it had never been, have robbed the delta of its once-rich wildlife and migratory birds.[8] Due to the rising level of salty water, foundations and sagging utility lines fill the landscape where there were once booming towns.

Likewise, the southern portions of the San Francisco Bay are severely polluted, both from the returned irrigation water (filled with chemicals and bacteria) entering from the Central Valley and from an ever-decreasing flow of freshwater entering the bay. The decline in the volume of the Sacramento River — due to irrigation in what would otherwise be a desert — allows more seawater to enter. This intrusion of salt water has changed the water's chemistry; consequently, native populations of sea life not attuned to heavily salted water — including the Dungeness crabs that once provided a livelihood for local fishermen — have declined. There have been many efforts to clean up the bay, but not much else can be done in the San Francisco–Berkeley–San Jose area — the depletion and pollution that take such a toll on the bay occur upstream in the Central Valley.

San Francisco has long looked to the Sierra Madre to provide water, and too much of that water has been, in the eyes of San Franciscans, diverted to agribusinesses in the Central Valley. Once, until the U.S. Bureau of Reclamation stepped in, San Francisco laid claim to literally all the snowmelt in the High Sierra. The dams, reservoirs, and canals sending that water to the Central Valley have meant that the water in the San Francisco Bay is heavily polluted. The San Francisco Bay Area is itself nationally renowned, as both a tourist destination and as a highly desirable place to live. The climate is moderate, the scenery striking, wages high, and unemployment low. (Recently, with the sinking of some computer software companies and a consequent decline of the wealth and influence of Silicon Valley, wages have been falling and unemployment rising, which will eventually lead to population stabilization.)[9] As San Francisco has run out of space, other areas around the bay have developed rapidly, including Berkeley, Oakland, and all of Silicon Valley (Palo Alto, Mountain View, San Jose, and other South Bay communities).[10] There are numerous cultural, social, and recreational attractions. All of these enticements have led to unparalleled population growth in the Bay Area, which has in turn led to many problems associated with such fast growth, including water shortages.

The water shortages can't be addressed locally or even regionally. The water must come from far away. So far, the Bay Area has looked for that water in the Sierra Nevada. But that water has many uses, and those uses are in conflict.

San Francisco versus the Hetch Hetchy Valley

"Dam Hetch Hetchy! As well dam for water-tanks the people's cathedrals and churches, for no holier temple has ever been consecrated by the heart of man."

So said John Muir, founder of the Sierra Club, in 1912. His fiery words appeared in newspapers from coast to coast. Muir described Hetch Hetchy (named after a type of grass that grew in that valley) as a "counterpart to Yosemite Valley" and extolled its virtues in several articles and books.[11] William Colby, also a protector of Muir's "range of light" — the Sierra Nevada — testified in a similar vein to the U.S. Congress. But their efforts were for naught: in 1913, the Congress voted to dam Yosemite's neighbor, and President Woodrow Wilson signed the bill into law. San Francisco's water czars had won. Hetch Hetchy Valley would become a lake. The Tuolumne River would be dammed, and the impounded water would inundate a portion of Yosemite National Park.

The O'Shaughnessy Dam was authorized and funded by the U.S. Congress in 1913, and construction was completed in 1923, thus submerging all of Hetch Hetchy Valley. But the war over this underwater valley has resurfaced. The Bay Area Water

Supply and Conservation Agency (BAWSCA) insists that the O'Shaughnessy Dam only needs to be refurbished to continue to supply water for the Bay Area. Others insist that it would be cheaper to demolish the dam and to rely on lower-elevation impoundments. The essential conflict has not changed since the early 1900s. The question then and the question now is: Should the water needs of a growing urban area take precedence over conserving natural areas?

The U.S. Congress struggled with this question from 1882 until 1913. The City of San Francisco made application to the U.S. Department of the Interior to dam the Hetch Hetchy Valley in 1902, but its application was denied. Only after many years of lobbying was the city able to persuade a reluctant Congress to allow it to dam up the Tuolumne River in Hetch Hetchy. Congress passed the Raker Bill (named after its sponsor, California's John E. Raker) by a contested vote.

The Raker Bill was a compromise: in exchange for being allowed to build the dam, the city had to generate electric power that would be sold directly to Bay Area citizens at the "cheapest possible rates." Otherwise, the grant of land in the Hetch Hetchy Valley would revert to the federal government. Consumer groups and newspapers have asserted for decades that the city has not complied with the "directly to the citizens" component of the Raker compromise. Instead, the electricity is sold to PG&E (Pacific Gas and Electric) at wholesale prices. PG&E then sells the electricity to local customers at retail rates. The city makes money, but PG&E makes much more. In spite of this seeming lack of compliance with the compromises in the Raker Act (the city argued and the federal courts concurred that PG&E was acting as an agent of the city), the lands of Hetch Hetchy remain under the control of the City of San Francisco — and the valley remains inundated.

The Sierra Club, John Muir's creation, continues to assert

that Yosemite National Park needs to be made whole again, by demolishing the O'Shaughnessy Dam and impounding the waters of the Tuolumne River downstream, outside Yosemite National Park. This notion has captured the attention of both the state and the federal governments, and a study is under way — with the San Francisco Board of Supervisors vowing to do whatever the study concludes — to determine whether this is feasible. More than a hundred years have passed since John Muir opposed the flooding of Hetch Hetchy; finally, during the Reagan administration, it was admitted that the Tuolumne River could be dammed downstream[12] to provide the same amount of water to San Francisco without inundating a valley in the Sierra.

Los Angeles versus Owens Valley

"Right over there," said Mark Reynolds,[13] "is where my grandfather had his farm. It's real sad to see all those dried-up stumps where the orchard once was. . . . But the farm had to be let go. Without water, well, it was just nothing. As you can see, the trees can't make it, cows can't make it, nothing can make it. Just dust."

Owens Valley, about 150 miles northeast of Los Angeles on the east side of the Sierra Madre, was described as a paradise with tall grasses, orchards, and farmlands watered by the Owens River.[14] Thanks to a gap in the Sierra Nevada that lets through storms from the Pacific, the mountains above Owens Valley receive a generous share of rainfall — more akin to the western slopes of the Sierra than the eastern. Once Mono Lake, at the head of the Owens River, was filled to the brim. Owens Lake was home to brine shrimp that fed millions of migratory birds. Owens Valley benefited from the water, the wildlife, and the fertile soil. Today the area is in a drastically different state. Mono Lake has dropped so much that eerie formations of calcium carbonate (called *tufa*) have been exposed. The Owens River has been drained dry as its flow has been diverted to Los Angeles. Owens Lake no longer has water; the migratory birds no longer visit the area, since no water also means no brine shrimp. Reynolds's grandfather's farm is filled with dry sand and sagebrush — and now even the sagebrush is dying. What was once, a mere eighty years ago, a productive and fertile agricultural area is now a weed-strewn desert, with the meager topsoil blowing away. The area is prone to enormous dust storms as the dried soil is captured by high winds off the Sierra. Only an Arctic dweller would consider Owens Valley a paradise.

What happened is simple.[15] Thanks to forward-thinking waterlords in Los Angeles — with a bit of complicity and perhaps even illegal actions by federal agencies — the distant City of Los Angeles simply took away all the water in Owens Valley. Every drop of water in the river and lake were transported to Los Angeles, and the city nearly drained Mono Lake (until a series of court decisions brought by a coalition of groups concerned about the condition of Mono Lake caused Los Angeles to "cease and desist." Los Angeles still takes water from the Owens River, but the court decisions essentially stated that enough water had to remain so that Mono Lake would not further decline).

By the 1930s, Los Angeles was firmly in control of all the water in Owens Valley. What had been a watery paradise turned into an arid hell. Now, thanks mostly to concerns of the U.S. Environmental Protection Agency about dust from the dry lakebed exceeding particulate standards, Los Angeles has instituted measures to convert the former lake from a dust bowl to a mud flat. Only a few small irrigated plots remain of what was once a huge agricultural area.

The outcome was predictable. The Los Angeles area was populous and growing. It contained rich and powerful people. Owens Valley, on the other hand, had a small, noninfluential population — it was quite literally a backwater that elected officials could ignore with impunity. Which they did, actively assisting Los Angeles in obtaining the water from Owens Valley. Los Angeles prospered and grew to the second-largest city in the United States. The small town and rural residents of Owens Valley, without water and hope, left.

Reynolds summed it up: "When everything became dry and dusty, my dad had no way of making a living. So he moved to Anaheim and took a job with the schools, driving a bus. We're still here, in Anaheim, drinking water, sprinkling the lawn, and filling up the pool. We've become part of the problem. Folks like us are the very reason that the Owens Valley is high and dry — no resources, no way to make money, no hope, no future. I look around here and all I see is dried-up dirt. It's hard to imagine that everything I'm looking at was once wet and prosperous. There's just nothing here. Nothing."

Slowly, we walked back to the car, and entered the highway (California 395) that would take us back to Los Angeles — land of glitter, glamour, and water. Losing the water war meant the end for Owens Valley, but it meant everything to the winners in Los Angeles. Now, however, thanks to people concerned about Mono Lake, the water war has continued and Los Angeles can claim, at this point, only a partial victory.

Los Angeles versus the Colorado River

Some of the water from Owens Valley still flows to Los Angeles — the court decisions allowed that — and Owens Valley remains desolate and dusty, as it was essentially abandoned when Los Angeles took the water. The pumps were pulled out, irrigation equipment rusted, and neither have been replaced. But in the 1920s the rapidly growing metropolitan area needed yet more water — more than Owens Valley was capable of supplying. For years, Los Angeles's water czars had eyed the Colorado River. The problem was that it was several hundred miles away, with a couple of mountain ranges and a forbidding desert in between.

Still, shortly after acquiring every drop of Owens Valley water in the early 1920s, Los Angeles began seriously investigating the Colorado River as a possible source of water. A drought and an expanding population had placed a strain on existing supplies. Building an aqueduct from the Colorado, however, would require more resources than the city could muster. Los Angeles then joined with several other communities, which were also seeking more water, to form the Metropolitan Water District of Southern California. Over the next decade, the district obtained voter approval to fund the project and constructed a network of pumping plants, reservoirs, and canals to bring water from Lake Havasu, behind the Bureau of Reclamation's Parker Dam, to the coastal plain. This water-diverting network, known as the Colorado River Aqueduct, took eight years to complete; the total distance the water travels from intakes at the Colorado's Parker Dam to the Los Angeles potable water treatment plant is 242 miles.

On completion of the Colorado River Aqueduct in 1941, the Metropolitan Water District began to wholesale Colorado River water to its member agencies. Today those agencies include fourteen cities, twelve municipal water districts, and a county water authority. More than 130 municipalities and many unincorporated areas are served by this project. Deliveries from the Colorado River began in June 1941, shortly after completion of the aqueduct. While the primary work was done during the depths of the Depression, when money was scarce, labor was cheap and readily available. The project employed thirty thousand people over an eight-year period — and as many as ten thousand people at one time — which made it Southern California's single largest work opportunity during the Depression.

Of course, the Metropolitan Water District took as much water as it could, leaving the Colorado River in a much-depleted state. "There ain't nothin' left. Down below there — that little green trickle — is all that's left of the biggest river around, maybe the biggest river in the West. But now look at it. You can wade across the whole damned thing and hardly get your feet wet," lamented Joe Hargrave, a longtime resident of Yuma, Arizona. "I can remember when sometimes it was wild and roaring — out of its banks. Other times, it was a bit quieter and not so rambunctious, but there was always plenty of water. But, you know, it was always kind of unusual. We don't get much rain here, but this river... it was kind of an oasis."

While Joe may have been engaging in a bit of hyperbole, the fact is that Yuma doesn't receive much rainfall (3 inches per year, on average), and so the Colorado River is its main source of water. But while on most occasions the river water is indeed a "greenish trickle," on other occasions, mostly when Mexico demands some portion of its share, the river returns to life and there is water from bank to bank. The Gila River runs out of Arizona and joins the Colorado River at Yuma. While the water in the Gila has also been claimed and re-claimed, occasionally, during times of desert rainfall, the Colorado and the Gila return to their glory days and run full and deep — not often, but often enough for Yuma to boast that it is a river town.[16] At other times, the Colorado River barely trickles, its waters removed by diversion to Los Angeles by the Colorado River Aqueduct.

The Colorado River at Yuma would probably always be a real river if it were not for the enormous appetites of the

Metropolitan Water District, the Imperial Valley, the Coachella Valley, the coastal city of San Diego, and the newly growing demands of Las Vegas and Phoenix. As it is, there's not much left for this river town. Yuma is in Arizona, and the Central Arizona Project uses Arizona's allocation under the Colorado River Compact. California uses more than its allocation, although the 1963 Supreme Court decision in *Arizona v. California* directed California to gradually cut back and take its allocated portion when all other states that were part of the compact used their full allocations. That time was reached in 1997.[17]

Las Vegas versus the Rest of Nevada (and, Eventually, Phoenix and Los Angeles, Too)

When the Colorado River Compact was approved by Nevada, officials from that basin state deemed the amount accorded Nevada appropriate. In the twenty-first century, however, with the rampant growth of Las Vegas, every drop of water authorized by the compact is taken by Nevada, and Las Vegas wants more. Right now, the battle for water among California, Phoenix, and Las Vegas is played out behind the scenes. All are reluctant to reopen the Colorado River Compact, for fear that negotiations would result in worsening a bad situation. But both Arizona and Nevada are taking their full allocations according to the agreements in the 1922 compact. Most of the water in Arizona flows to Phoenix through the Central Arizona Project, and most of the water to Nevada flows to Las Vegas, via Lake Mead pipelines. California has been taking more than its share but has promised to cut back and take only what is authorized.

On the face of it, the cities of Las Vegas and Phoenix have much in common. Both are located at sites that once provided plenty of water — but for much smaller populations. The translation of *Las Vegas* is "the meadows," so named for the springs that kept grasses green and plentiful way back in the early 1900s. Phoenix is at the junction of the Verde and Gila rivers. Both are among the fastest-growing cities in this country,[18] with developments sprawling in all directions. Because vast arid, sandy plains surround them, they have plenty of room to expand. Summertime temperatures are uncomfortably high. Both cities have long outgrown the water available: The Las Vegas springs no longer reach the surface because of capping and overuse due to groundwater pumping. The water in the Verde and Gila rivers was long ago appropriated by Phoenix. Both are now looking everywhere for additional sources. That search has led to bitter struggles for the waters of the Colorado.

Las Vegas is arguably the better known of the two cities, offering a vast array of activities, from outrageous to tame. When you walk down the Strip in Vegas, you find a line of glittering palaces, and everywhere fountains, pools, and waterfalls. There are copious amounts of water in the desert. Green lawns, pools, and golf courses sparkle and shimmer. While not as major a tourist destination, Phoenix has its own golf course habits. Everywhere, you find greenery in a naturally brown land.

In a time of water shortages, high heat, and little rainfall (both Phoenix and Las Vegas have recently experienced record-setting temperatures; the entire area is undergoing a prolonged drought) — and in recognition that the profligate use of water cannot continue — Phoenix has imposed some meager conservation efforts on water usage, as has Las Vegas. These efforts have mostly taken the form of various incentives for converting green lawns to brown ones. Otherwise, there seems to be no nod toward the reality of living in a land of little rain. Phoenix long ago exhausted its surface water and groundwater, having pumped water out of the underlying aquifer until there was nothing left. In the past, several reservoirs on the Verde and Gila rivers helped Phoenix's water problem somewhat, but it was the Central Arizona Project that has allowed this high and dry city to become water rich.

The Colorado River Compact specifies that Arizona, as a "Lower Basin" state, has a right to 2.8 million acre-feet of water per year. However, that water is not always available due to low flow levels on the Colorado River. The idea behind the Central Arizona Project is that in flush years, Arizona would take every drop to which it was entitled and store it somewhere for use in dry years.[19] The first problem was determining the "somewhere," and that was resolved when it was discovered that an immense underground area — which had been pumped dry — was available. A secondary, but equally difficult, problem was how to get the water from the Colorado River to where it was needed in Arizona. Phoenix is considerably lower in elevation than the Colorado River, but the water would need to be pumped out of the river basin and over mountain ranges. Not having the wherewithal to construct all the dams, diversions, aqueducts, pumps, and pipes, Phoenix turned to the state politicians. Arizona's congressional representatives and senators had secured seats on committees that had much to do with water projects, and the money was appropriated for the U.S. Bureau of Reclamation to begin construction on an elaborate system that would draw water from Lake Havasu on the Arizona-California border (and a reservoir on the Colorado River) and deliver this water to the central city of Phoenix and the southern city of Tucson. In the arcane language of Congress, the project was for "Indian and non-Indian" lands. But Native Americans saw little of the water; most of it went to support the needs of rapid growth in Phoenix with a smattering to other locales, including Tucson and Prescott. Thanks to the federal government and some well-placed and persistent

Arizona legislators, Phoenix is relatively well heeled at present, as its water needs go. However, it cannot continue growing on its current supply.

Las Vegas's present population is estimated at 2.8 million. "It's going to race toward 3 million," says Geoff Schumacher, who wrote *Sun, Sin & Suburbia: An Essential History of Modern Las Vegas*. In an interview with the *Pahrump Valley Times*, of Nye County, Nevada, Schumacher predicted that Las Vegas would continue to grow. The article reports:

> The population is expected to hit the 3.5 million mark by 2026. Like putting in wider highways, people and traffic always seem to overtake the infra- structure available.
>
> Schumacher doesn't think the lack of water will ever limit Las Vegas' growth, though the percentage of growth will doubtless diminish over time, he says.
>
> "Las Vegas has money, and money buys water. The money is just going to flow, and they want the water to flow in return."
>
> Schumacher was referring to plans for a federally approved pipeline delivering water to Las Vegas from Lincoln and White Pine counties. He says, "If I had one piece of advice for rural Nevada, I would say, 'Demand money.'
>
> "If Las Vegas didn't have the money, Las Vegas would dry up in 10 years."
>
> But residents need to understand the economic forces at play in Nevada and in the nation. "It's part of a much more ominous situation," Schumacher says. People are moving here from the East, the Midwest and California to find the American Dream that once was met by Los Angeles.

Now, it's places like Las Vegas.... "It's part of a bigger migration," he says. People are seeking a sunny climate in which to live.[20]

Las Vegas is now in the position that Phoenix was, in that the city is rapidly growing but doesn't have the water resources to support such growth. Located in the Lower Basin, as defined by the Colorado River Compact, Nevada and, by extension, Las Vegas, doesn't get much water from the Colorado River. Recognizing that it would be difficult to divvy up the Upper Basin allotment by acre-feet, due to the erratic amount of waters available in the Colorado River from year to year, the Upper Basin states went instead for percentages. The Lower Basin, however, did the opposite and assigned specific acre-feet allotments to each state. Nevada got the short end of the stick, since the water appropriated to each state was done so on the basis of "irrigable" land.[21] Nevada didn't have much of that, and therefore it must get along on a measly amount of the Colorado River's water — about 300,000 acre-feet per year. The needs of Clark County, where Las Vegas is situated, exceed that already, although the amount allotted does provide a baseline supply of Las Vegas's water.

Pat Mulroy, the likable and outspoken water czarina for Las Vegas, threatened to reopen the Colorado River Compact in order to address the changing needs in the Upper and Lower basins. The other states that signed the 1922 compact didn't like that idea, for fear that it would lead not only to prolonged negotiations but also to new winners and losers. Finding herself alone with little or no support from anyone outside Nevada, Mulroy initiated conservation efforts that paid citizens to stop watering their lawns, for example, and encouraged the use of recycled water in decorative fountains and waterfalls. She then began looking around for sources of water to slake her city's thirst.

The latest proposal from Mulroy is to pump groundwater from White Pine County in northern Nevada and transport it to Las Vegas.[22] While this proposal has its share of opponents and will take years to be resolved, Las Vegas, for the time being, has laid aside any further claims on Colorado River water. Mulroy, however, has spoken out: "Things have changed, but what remains the same is that California was the problem back then [in 1922], and California is the problem today."[23] Mulroy was referring to California's consistent practice of taking more water than the Colorado River Compact entitled it to; she was also vaguely threatening to reopen the Colorado River Compact, a threat that sent shivers down the spines of elected officials in all Colorado River basin states. However, the U.S. Supreme Court had directed California to use its allocation, and no more, when the other basin states used their full allocations. Reopening the Colorado River Compact would entail each basin state's asserting its needs above those of all other basin states — and would eventually bring the Las Vegas–Phoenix squabble into the open.

If, however, the proposal to pump groundwater from the nether regions of Nevada doesn't succeed, then Mulroy will have little choice but to turn to the Colorado River for more water — and make demands on California's share. Mulroy must find water in order for her city to continue to grow. When and if she looks south toward Lake Mead, the Colorado River Compact will be reopened and appropriations renegotiated. At that time, Los Angeles, Phoenix, and Las Vegas will be vying for the same water. The smoldering feuds will become conflagrations, and the Colorado River will likely be asked to deliver more than it can (see chapter 1, "Taking What Is Not There"). If any new compact is based on reality, the cities of the desert — Las Vegas, Phoenix — may well be forced to accept that reality and to curtail population growth by limiting water resources and restricting subdivision development.

The Heartland: Upstream versus Downstream on the Missouri River

The Missouri River watershed is immense, draining the eastern and middle sections of the Rocky Mountains, all of the northern plains, and major portions of Kansas, Iowa, and Missouri. Yet in some places, the Missouri is a river no more. Thanks to human manipulations during the past century, there are at least four separate segments of the Missouri River,[24] with the far segment upstream in Montana and the lowest one downstream at the river's confluence with the Mississippi, in St. Charles County, Missouri. From Great Falls, Montana, to St. Louis, Missouri, the waters of the Missouri River are involved in an upstream-downstream battle, and the river itself is subject to changes in management by the U.S. Army Corps of Engineers, the entity charged by Congress to manage the river. In an attempt to balance all the competing interests, the corps tried to appease everyone. But as it attempts to manage any of these four segments, the corps inevitably and often negatively affects the other segments. As one Iowa farmer (who could care less, because his lands are not in the Missouri River floodplains), told me, "It looks to me as if they tried to give something to everybody, but instead of making everybody happy, they just pissed off everybody."[25]

The modern Missouri River is no longer the river that Lewis and Clark saw back in the early 1800s, when it was a free-flowing and natural watercourse, described as "braided and meandering."[26] In William Least Heat-Moon's book *River-Horse*, in which he recounts traveling the United States via its waterways, he describes occasions on which he was unable to determine the main channel of the Missouri, often finding himself bottomed out, surrounded by cattails and reeds.

In the current feud, the upstream states of Montana, the Dakotas, and Nebraska want the Missouri's large reservoirs to be stabilized at optimal levels. They define *optimal* as beneficial to a burgeoning fishing industry, with nods to irrigation and drinking-water intakes. Any untimely drawdowns, some say any drawdowns at all, result in miles of mudflats — and fishing resorts, boat docks, and launch ramps on dry land. Tumbleweeds that thrive on the exposed flats have rolled into small prairie towns and collected on the walls of buildings, posing real fire hazards.

Downstream interests — the states of Kansas, Iowa, and, in particular, Missouri — want waters released from the upstream dams to enhance commercial navigation, which is seen as beneficial to agricultural interests. Farmers, farm groups, and the governmental offices of the State of Missouri are adamantly opposed to any releases of water that might add to spring flooding.[27] In a nod to those concerns, the Army Corps of Engineers placed in the Master Manual a section that stated there would be no release from the upstream reservoirs that would add to spring flooding and, conversely, added another section stating that no release would be forthcoming if the upstream reservoirs were low.

At the same time that it must juggle these competing interests, the corps is under pressure from the U.S. Fish and Wildlife Service, Native American tribes, and environmental and conservation organizations to take the steps called for by the federal Endangered Species Act.[28] While several species dependent on the Missouri River and its floodplains have been labeled endangered by the secretary of the interior, it is the pallid sturgeon that has caused the so-called spring rise. The Fish and Wildlife Service has stated that the sturgeons in the downstream segment of the Missouri will spawn in response to increased waters in the late spring. This is apparently based on records that show a rise in waters due to snowmelt and runoff from the northern plains.

In an attempt to appease upstream interests, the corps,

in a required revision of the Master Manual, agreed to draw down the large reservoirs on a rotating basis. In this way, the engineers reasoned, five of the six impoundments would be maintained at levels deemed optimal by the upstreamers.

Downstream groups immediately opposed this proposal, because it would mean that, after high water in the spring, the Missouri would not be navigable by barges in the fall.[29] Autumn, it is argued, is when barges are needed to transport harvested grains. The corps made no concession to this but instead proposed two spring rises: one in March, which would emulate the snowmelt and spring rains in the northern plains, and the other in late May or early June to mimic snowmelt from the Rockies. Duplication of the historical hydrograph, the corps and the Fish and Wildlife Service asserted, would prevent the extinction of an endangered species.

Farmers in the floodplains of the lower river — Iowa, Kansas, and particularly Missouri — asserted that releases of water in the spring would jeopardize the acres of soybeans and corn and might or might not lead to a greater population of sturgeon. They have stated consistently that before tinkering with the Big Muddy, the corps needs to be certain that the spring rise will result in spawning by the pallid sturgeon, and that their crops should not be sacrificed in conducting an experiment, since no one is certain whether a spring rise will succeed in triggering a mating urge in the pallid sturgeon. Lower Basin river management hearings sponsored by the corps have been contentious and raucous — with farmers and their supporters among the state's elected and appointed officials claiming that the corps was set to flood their crops.[30]

This upstream-downstream conflict has been going on for more than a hundred years.[31] In 1940, construction was completed on the Fort Peck Dam in upstream eastern Montana to allow the storage of water that could be released to ensure a sufficient flow (or depth) for barges downstream on the lower Missouri. During the period of construction, Montanans did not object to construction of this dam, since they would get the benefits of construction jobs and a lake that would benefit tourism. Immediately after the construction ended, Montanans began objecting: the jobs were gone and the lake behind Fort Peck Dam was not suitable for tourism because of its considerable fluctuations in response to downstream needs. Farther downstream, the massive Lake Sacajawea (actually a reservoir) near Williston, North Dakota, has become so filled with sediment that the upper reaches of this impoundment consist of little more than marshes and wetlands. Reeds and other water plants and migratory birds thrive in this habitat, but fish and fishing boats haven't fared as well. North Dakotans feel they are stuck with all the liabilities of supporting downstream commercial navigation but receive very few benefits. Akin to the reservoir impounded behind the Fort Peck Dam, Lake Sacajawea has never supported tourism, and the buildup of sediment (combined with constantly fluctuating water levels) rules out any future tourist attractions.

While the upstream dams were constructed by the Army Corps of Engineers to support commercial navigation — barge traffic on the lower river — below Sioux City, that barge traffic peaked in 1975, and even at its peak it was well below the corps' estimate. Since 1975, barge traffic on the Missouri River declined each year,[32] until in 2005 it disappeared altogether. A towboat pilot told me that the Big Muddy was just too hard to navigate while pushing (towboats don't tow on the Missouri — they push) a quarter mile of barges: "The current is just too swift. Going downstream, you'd think it would be easy, just go with the flow. But it's worse going downstream than it is to go up. The problem is that it flows too fast and the channel wanders back and forth. To avoid running up on a sandbar or onto a wing dam, you've got to keep the engines in reverse — you've got to go slower than the current to keep control. Even then, it's hard. I've been on the Mississippi and the Ohio. Those are easy — all those long deep pools and then the locks at the dams that raise the tows and the barges up and down. But, you know, as long as the Missouri is managed to be a deep, swift channel, it'll never make it for moving stuff."[33]

And indeed it hasn't. After the corps rejected an earlier proposal to release water in the late summer and early fall, several barge companies announced that they would no longer operate on the Missouri.[34] Their given reasons were that the water depth was not dependable and the short season not economically viable. But the U.S. Congress — led by Missouri's delegation — continues to ignore this reality of no commercial navigation and requires the corps to keep a 9-foot navigational channel from Sioux City to the confluence. The corps does as it is told by federal law and the U.S. Congress, though there is documentation that suggests the corps makes recommendations to Congress and then Congress affirms those recommendations by ordering the corps to do what the corps has recommended.[35] It is definitely in the interests of downstream state and federal officials to pretend that barge traffic continues to exist, and the corps is sensitive to those interests. The Missouri Farm Bureau and the levee districts don't pretend. In constructing the wing dams, bank stabilizations, and channelization, the corps not only tamed the Big Muddy but also created (or caused to accrete) more than 100,000 acres of rich and fertile farmland in the Missouri River Valley from Rulo, Nebraska, to St. Charles, Missouri. In this manner, the navigational channel is kept in place in order that the corps' towboats and barges can transport rocks and repair wing dams for a nonexistent barge industry (and, coincidentally, protect the accreted farmland). In essence, the corps ends up maintaining the river for itself. The fight over who gets what, and when, goes on. In the meantime, miles and miles of mudflats surround upstream reservoirs; where there is water in the reservoirs, it is filled with sediment; the barge industry has given up on operating on the Missouri; and taxpayer money goes to support all of this.

Dixieland Water Woes

In the well-watered area of the southeastern United States, the states of Florida, Georgia, and Alabama struggle over waters in the basins of the Chattahoochee, Flint, and Apalachicola rivers. At issue is essentially who gets how much water and what will be done with it.[36]

The State of Georgia wants the waters of the Chattahoochee River and its impoundment, Lake Lanier, for the burgeoning city of Atlanta. Without that water, Georgia officials assert, Atlanta will run dry.[37] Florida is concerned about how much water Georgia plans to leave in the Chattahoochee River, which joins the Flint River at Lake Seminole to flow into Florida's Apalachicola River and into the oyster-rich Apalach-icola Bay. Alabama is stuck in the middle, not growing nearly as fast as Georgia and Florida but wanting its share for drinking, industry, recreation, and other uses that were spelled out in the August 2003 Memorandum of Understanding among the three states. Florida claims that Georgia broke the agreement before the ink was hardly dry, and Alabama has joined Florida in this assertion.

The battle has reached a fever peak, even reaching the White House. At one point, Alabama's two U.S. senators placed a "hold" (for unspecified reasons, but presumably to send a message to Georgia and Florida) on a White House nominee to the Army Corps of Engineers. The State of Florida filed suit in federal court against the State of Georgia in 2003, and in 2005 Florida appealed a decision that went against it.

From Pennsylvania Avenue to Peachtree Street, the battle over the area's waters has at times more closely resembled a street brawl than a dignified discourse among affected states, involving rash and accusatory media statements by public officials, the refusal of Alabama's U.S. senators to accede to a presidential appointment, and the alleged violation by one or more states of a negotiated agreement. A water war is not at all what one would expect to encounter in an area that receives somewhere around 60 inches of precipitation each year (Atlanta receives about 51 inches). Yet the booming population growth of the area has placed a great deal of stress on the area's rivers, to the point that once-placid tidewater rivers have become a bone of contention among these states. Jeb Bush, the governor of Florida, said in September 2003 (shortly after the Memorandum of Understanding was signed): "This state would ask federal courts to decide how the rivers would be split, rather than continuing to submit to the federally sanctioned water compact negotiations." Sonny Perdue, the governor of Georgia, shot back that "Florida has kind of gone on their own way."

Lost in this war of words was what it would mean for water in Atlanta, the cities and towns of the Florida Panhandle, and the terrestrial and aquatic animals that depend on a constant flow in the Apalachicola River. While each state asserted its needs, each side forgot or ignored the needs of the others. Rather than participate in good-faith negotiations, the officials of Florida and Georgia went to a court of law and asked it to decide the fate of the water in the Apalachicola River. While Florida has "won" and Georgia has "lost," it is indicative of a much larger problem that two seemingly well-watered states are bickering over water.

New York and the Catskills

For the past hundred years or so, New York City has depended on reservoirs in the Catskills of upper New York State for its water supply.[38] A series of reservoirs in the Catskill Mountains are connected to the city by a complex of pumps, pipes, and aquifers. The watersheds of the reservoirs are pristine, as is the water. In fact, the water provided to New Yorkers from these reservoirs is so pure that no treatment or removal of contaminants is necessary to make it fit for human consumption. Thus, the water arrives at each faucet direct from the reservoirs.

The relationship between New York City and the small towns of the Catskills has always been slightly contentious. Locals have asserted that New York City has taken and inundated the best lands in the Catskills so that New Yorkers may luxuriate in long showers. This below-the-surface tension has steadily increased as tourism in the Catskills has declined over the past few decades. The area has been looking for quite some time for ways to return to the plush times of its tourist-heavy yesteryear. Riding into this high unemployment and low-wage vacuum was a development group, Crossroads,[39] with many investors from around the country but headed by local hotelier Dean Gitter, who had a proposal he claimed would rejuvenate tourism in the Catskills.

The development company, by Dean Gitter's estimation, has already spent more than $20 million in paperwork between 1998 and 2004 in responding to information required by the State of New York. What is proposed is truly large scale: included are two 18-hole golf courses, two hotels with a total of 400 rooms, 351 time-share units, 832 bedrooms in "additional buildings" (perhaps cabins), retail stores, recreational facilities, clubhouses, a luxury housing development, maintenance buildings, roads, parking lots, a sewage treatment plant, and a temporary cement plant. The complex would contain two tracts: one in Delaware County (the west complex) and one in Ulster County (the east complex). Altogether, the land subject to manipulation would comprise 1,960 acres.

However, according to New York City water department staff and various local consumer and conservation groups, the proposed golf resort and lodging complex threaten the quality and quantity of the city's water supply. The U.S. Environmental Protection Agency has informed the city that if the quality of water cannot be guaranteed, the city would need to build a large treatment facility, which would cost around $6 billion. Although the first concern is the possible contamination of New York City's drinking water, which supplies more than nine million people, there is also concern that the complex will suck up so much water that local communities will run dry.

After five years of work by the developers, consultants, and contractors, a draft environmental impact statement was submitted to the state's Department of Environmental Conservation. This document of several thousand pages was promptly challenged by several conservation groups and the City of New York. The department referred the entire matter to an administrative law judge, who, in 2005 issued a 167-page decision. Essentially, the judge found twelve areas in which the draft environmental impact statement was deficient and declined to issue any permits to the developer. Immediately the development company appealed that decision.

At that point, Maurice Hinchey, the congressional representative of the Adirondacks area, proposed that the complex be cut in half — that the west portion be built as planned, but that the east portion be abandoned, and the lands ceded to the State of New York as an addition to Catskills Park. Dean Gitter responded, quite assertively, in the negative. Hinchey stuck by his proposal and added to it.[40] According to a report in the *Phoenicia Times*,

He said that the impact of paving 85 acres of forest land and removing hundreds of thousands of trees to build the resort would "produce storm-water runoff that would severely threaten the quality of New York City Watershed and increase the potential for serious flooding. It would also generate a substantial increase in traffic throughout the Route 28 corridor, strain public services, burden area taxpayers and threaten the integrity of the Catskill Mountain Preserve." He said this would cause New York City to be required to build a multi-billion dollar filtration plant. "If the quality of the water in the New York City Watershed declines to the point where a filtration system is needed, it will unnecessarily cost taxpayers billions of dollars. We can prevent that from ever happening if we put our foot down and resist development that endangers the Watershed. And by protecting New York City's water supply, you protect Kingston's reservoirs and people's individual wells. Water is the most precious resource known to humanity. With a development like this, the issue of filtration takes precedence. If it went through, there is little doubt the EPA would order filtration. $6 billion and [it] will go up, plus a half billion a year for operations. Those are very large sums of money borne by New York City and state taxpayers."[41]

Dean Gitter was not budging. The *Phoenicia Times* report cited above quoted Gitter as saying:

"We have planned for 10 years something which we think is financeable. Golf is an amenity, without profit, in itself. It increases the utility of a hotel. Skiing is also an amenity, and they logically compliment [sic] each other." He said that the Catskills, as an attraction, are stuck with old notions. "The Catskills are not a favorable destination. You have to hit the top of the market and the middle of the market. Wildacres (the Western portion of the proposal) is the middle. The Big Indian Spa (the eastern side, which Hinchey wants to eliminate) is an extension of the Emerson. If you build the top of the line world class facility, the world will respond. The top of the market is what sets the tone. When you have opinion makers and news makers, then the middle market follows behind it. It's topographically impossible to do both in Wildacres. Big Indian is a spectacular site, and it's private land."

As Gitter appealed, conservation organizations added six more issues that the court will need to address. It may be many, many years before the resort proposal sinks or swims according to the cold dictates of some final court. While land use is one of the main issues of contention, the real issue is water: who gets how much and in what condition. New Yorkers agree that the developer must be stopped in order to prevent the depletion and pollution of that city's water supply, and folks in the Adirondacks are equally opposed. Most of the Adirondack dwellers live in the area in order to avoid golf courses, condos, and large resort hotels. Some local town officials have publicly stated support for the Belleayre Resort project,[42] but those officials have taken heat from local opponents. At this time, Gitter has few friends.

[WHAT YOU CAN DO]

In a work of fiction by John Nichols, *The Milagro Bean-field War,* Joe Mondragon, a farmer in the mountains of New Mexico whose beanfield was wilting in the sun due to a lack of water, took matters into his own hands and shoveled open a water-filled acequia, or canal, to irrigate his beans. Having started what is known as the Milagro Beanfield War,[43] Mondragon's simple act of defiance made him the target of influential resort owners and state politicians. He was hounded, harassed, shot at, and jailed, but he persevered and — remember, this is a work of fiction — was eventually exonerated.

While diverting a few hundred gallons of water is still possible, it is not possible to divert hundreds of acre-feet that flow through concrete-lined aqueducts or huge pipes. Today, the vast majority of decisions about our water supply are made in the back rooms of city hall, state capitols, and the House and Senate office buildings in our nation's capital. No individual citizens allowed, unless you have the largesse for entry. That was the case with the acquisition of Owens Valley water by Los Angeles; it was the case with the damming of Hetch Hetchy Valley by San Francisco; and it is the case in the water feuds in New York, the Missouri River basin, the Apalachicola watershed, and the Colorado and Rio Grande basins.

As we've seen in this chapter, particularly in the cases of the Catskills and the downstream areas of the Missouri River, citizens occasionally band together and disrupt the backroom decisions. Such was the case in the proposed revision of the Missouri River Master Manual. In public hearings on the revision, groups of downstream farmers organized and spoke with one voice. While that voice may have been a self-interested one, the Army

Corps of Engineers felt it could not ignore that outcry and made several concessions. Likewise, in the water feud in New York, several bands of concerned citizens became involved, opposed the Belleayre Resort in the media, in demonstrations, and in the litigation. While the involvement of these New York residents may or may not have made a difference, they could not be ignored. As yet, no citizens' groups have become involved in reallocating Colorado River water, although there has been some involvement by environmental organizations in Las Vegas's development. It is fairly certain that, were it not for citizens becoming involved in the water woes of Phoenix, the city would not now require a hundred-year guarantee of water for new subdivisions.

Several national organizations are involved in water issues from San Francisco to New York. Local individual involvement is critical. Please contact one or more of these organizations:

- The Sierra Club
- Public Citizen
- Natural Resources Defense Council (NRDC)
- Environmental Working Group
- Clean Water Network (also involved with water-quantity issues)

In each of the water wars discussed in this chapter, the sanctity of our water supply, our environment, and human welfare hangs in the balance. Each side believes it's right, but unfortunately not all sides are thinking about the long-term viability of our water supply. Thus, we must each be vocal about our stance for the health of our environment — which determines our own health and quality of life — over industry, over wealth, and over expansion.

Of course, when economic growth and the livelihoods of several million people are at stake, it is difficult for any one person to have much influence — and rightly so. However, if that person's views are shared by several hundred, and those several hundred join with others of like mind to form coalitions of several thousand, appointed and elected officials are more likely to heed their advice. Likewise, it is financially difficult for one person to hire banks of attorneys knowledgeable about water laws. But it is completely possible for organizations of citizens to hire such attorneys to assist in negotiations and to litigate if necessary.

Therefore, if we don't like to see entire valleys dewatered and decimated, and we don't want to see a huge resort in an otherwise pristine area, and we want to protect and preserve wildlife and aquatic habitat, we must lend the support of our voices — in the form of donations, petition signings, and letters to newspaper editors and politicians — to the local, regional, and national organizations fighting to preserve what water we have left. As the 1960s slogan goes, If you're not part of the solution, you're part of the problem.

five

PRIVATIZATION

The Risks of Putting Our Water Supply into Corporate Hands

While the previous chapter detailed the major U.S. water wars, a quieter but equally bitter battle is going on around the country between a number of municipal water utilities and the for-profit companies hired by the cities to run their water delivery systems. As water supplies dwindle and aging infrastructures make delivery difficult, private water companies have stepped in, seeing opportunities for profit where cities see only problems. While the initial contract negotiations between cities and private industry took place behind closed doors, the increasingly poor quality of the water being delivered to the area's faucets, combined with rising rates for that water, has captured the residents' attention. The central question on all sides is "Whose water is it?"

At the recent World Water Forum in Mexico City, people marched in the streets, protesting the drinking-water systems that have been taken over by private companies. They were specifically advocating that water delivery systems be publicly — not privately — owned and managed. Seventeen activists were apprehended by the Mexican Public Security Agency (a counterpart to the FBI). The activists knew that arrests were likely but felt so strongly about water being publicly owned and managed that they were willing to make that sacrifice.[1]

While the privatization of water has caused considerable consternation, controversy, and outcry throughout the world, this issue has not led to national headlines in the United States or to any arrests. However, the issue has become front-page news in areas where water privatization has caused problems. A thousand or so U.S. cities have implemented water privatization.[2] Water companies say that the number is higher and assert that privatization creates only a few problems and that the vast majority of private companies do well; concerned citizens say that the number is lower and assert that problems are rife and systemic; in any case, privatized agreements have become the fodder for initiative petitions, litigation, and attempts to terminate contracts. The issues are the same as those in Mexico — poor water quality, rising rates, a belief that the supply and delivery of water should be publicly controlled. The public outcry in the United States has been directed mostly at elected officials who've "sold" public ownership and management. As other areas of the country begin to experience water shortages and problems with aging infrastructures, it is likely that more areas will resort to privatization and that more citizens and corporate water companies will become more embroiled in controversies.

Water is absolutely essential to life. The human body is estimated to be about 60 percent water.[3] Neglecting to drink enough water will quickly cause dehydration and death in humans. As desert dwellers, hikers, and backpackers will attest, it is possible to go for many days without food — but only for a day or two without water. The United Nation's World Heath Organization has calculated that each person requires 50 liters per day (about 6 gallons) to meet basic human needs, primarily for drinking and cooking. Anything above those 50 liters is a "want," not a need. Yet in the United States, the average per-person daily consumption is about 50 gallons, or 200 liters.[4]

Privatization's Greatest Successes and Failures

The one thing that the beautiful Low Country islands near Charleston, South Carolina, cannot boast about is the taste of the water. Reverse osmosis, a type of filtering system, is required to remove the offending taste and odor of what comes out of every faucet. While a few hardy folks do permanently reside in the Low Country island communities sprinkled between Myrtle Beach, South Carolina, and Savannah, Georgia — in spite of mosquitoes, high humidity, and stifling summer heat

— most of the residences are vacation homes or rentals. From the upscale housing and living conditions at Hilton Head to somewhat more modest conditions at Edisto Island, people from far and wide are attracted to the marshes and the ocean. There has been development, to be sure, but for the most part, the marshes are protected and preserved.

The Low Country islands, in their zeal to attract tourists, boast of the ocean views; wildlife watching; fresh fish, oysters, crabs, and shrimp; sea breezes; marsh scenery; and various festivals. But nowhere in their tourist brochures is there mention of the water itself. Part of the problem is that the Low Country communities are barely above sea level, and even deep wells tap into brackish water. While the water treatment plants remove various contaminants to ensure that drinking-water standards are met, the taste and odor remain. "Blecchh" is the most common response to drinking water from the tap. While it is suitable for bathing, watering the lawn, and washing clothes, it is barely potable. Even cooking and making coffee is best done with water that has been "strained" through a reverse osmosis system.

While the desirability of the water in this area is low, the infrastructure that brings it into homes and businesses is just fine. Water is delivered without fail, and while normal maintenance and operation costs are incurred, there are no failing pipes. Because most of the water systems along the southeastern coast were installed within the past 50 years, there has not been time for dilapidation and failure.

This means that, while the water is unpalatable, there are no reasons for communities to turn to private water companies, and conversely, there is no reason for a private water company to "cut a deal" with any of these communities. There is very little profit in a massive reverse osmosis system — especially when private homeowners, and some communities, have installed their own systems for drinking purposes. Many kitchen sinks have a third handle in addition to the hot and cold faucets. That third handle turns on the water from the reverse osmosis system under the sink. Usually small, the in-home treatment system can handle 50 or more gallons per day. Fifty gallons will quench the thirst of several people, and very seldom is the capacity of a home system exceeded. Thus there is no need for community water systems to invite bids from private water companies — the need simply isn't present.

This was not the case in Atlanta.[5] By 2002, the water delivery infrastructure was at least a hundred years old and in need of major and costly repairs. Low-income residences in the central city had problems, true. But the real crisis occurred when the relatively rich residents of the Buckhead neighborhood began experiencing rusty or discolored water from their taps and boil orders became frequent. Boil orders are issued by the city or state health department — or the Safe Drinking Water agency — when drinking the local water might be harmful. Rather than call for a bond issue, which would have raised water rates (rates which will now have to be raised, anyway), the city council instead signed a contract with a private water company. The company committed to making the infrastructure repairs while continuing to deliver untainted water on a reliable basis — without any significant raise in rates. The water company had done the math and decided that it could make money (profit was the primary motive, as with all corporate endeavors) while doing the necessary repairs.

Unfortunately, the system fell apart. Shortly after the private company took over Atlanta's water delivery system in 2000, repairs and replacements of failing pipes got under way, stirring up contaminants that then entered the water supply. Repairs knocked rust loose from the decaying pipes, resulting in water of even poorer quality coming from kitchen sinks and shower heads. As pipes were replaced, water was shut off until the newer pipes were in place, and contaminants such as bacteria were feared to have entered the stagnant water system, resulting in boil orders. In addition, the number of major repairs that were necessary had been vastly underestimated. The city claimed that the company had been aware that a significant overhaul was needed; the company claimed that the city had not revealed that the entire system was failing.

In any event, the contract between the private water company and the City of Atlanta was finally terminated — with each side blaming the other. The situation has returned to some degree of normalcy. Boil orders are down significantly, and the water flowing from taps is pure and clean. There are still unresolved problems with Atlanta's water system — ones that will need to be resolved "some day." In the meantime, the City of Atlanta judged that it was better to deal with the problems itself, rather than depend on a private company to make the necessary upgrades. While rates would go up, at least the increase would be used to make necessary repairs, not to fill corporate coffers. Since the water company was a for-profit entity, its first concern was believed to be making a profit.[6] Well down the list of corporate priorities was the satisfactory delivery of services — pure, clean, and abundant water. Unfortunately, in delivering unsatisfactory water, the company lost the contract and any profit it had hoped to gain.

"You know, I had never even thought about it," commented Angela Woodall, a resident of Jesup, Georgia, who spends much time in Atlanta, where she works. "In my office, you turn on the tap, or flush the john — and there's water. You just take it for granted. I didn't even know that a private company had been contracted to take over Atlanta's water system, until all of a sudden what came out of the tap was sort of rust colored. Then almost every day, there was an order — from the Health Department or someone — to boil water before drinking it. And you're thinking, What the hell happened? What we once took for granted — clean water — became a real luxury.

"I tell you what," she went on. "It'll be a long time before anyone in this city takes water for granted. That United Water company just flat-out messed up our water. They violated almost everything in their contract. The city folks didn't really have a choice — they were catching grief from all directions. So the contract was terminated. Maybe the city will have to raise rates. United Water would have had to do the same, or their profit margin would have been sucking mud." She laughed. "And the rest of us would have been drinking mud."

Angela's comments, while exaggerated (the water company, for example, did not violate "almost everything in their contract"), capture the fear among those citizens who view such privatization as encroaching on an essential human right. According to the nonprofit organization Public Citizen, if widespread privatization occurs, the communities affected will be at the mercy of a for-profit entity for their most essential, life-sustaining product.[7] Since profit is the driving force, if profit suffers or is not deemed sufficient to award shareholders, then the company will threaten to withhold water in an effort to raise rates. At that point, a basic human need will be held hostage to the profit motive. That describes exactly the fear of citizens in Stockton, California; Lexington, Kentucky; and, of course, Atlanta.

In Stockton, California, on the other side of the continent from Atlanta, water privatization again became the subject of a major controversy.[8] The Stockton City Council, in the face of community opposition, signed a contract with a European-based water company. That the city council did this was mystifying to several community groups, which organized in opposition. According to these groups, the municipal water utility was financially sound, and there had been no major difficulties with water quality. The only reason given by the city council was that the private company could manage water supply and delivery more efficiently than the city could. A contract was signed, in spite of a citizen petition, to turn the water system over to OMI/Thames. This move was immediately followed by prolonged but eventually successful litigation. The State of California requires an environmental study (similar to the federally required environmental impact statement), and the circuit court judge ruled — after standing and summary judgment issues were decided or dismissed — that such a study must include real alternatives, not just foregone conclusions. The contract was voided in 2005.[9]

While it did not work for Atlanta or Stockton, water privatization is not always disastrous. Many cities have long turned to private companies to manage their water delivery systems. Indianapolis has had such a system in place for more than a hundred years. As noted earlier, more than a thousand American communities — large, medium, and small — have contracted with private companies that are responsible for all aspects of delivering water to residents. Very few of those communities, however, have turned over their water supplies — the source water itself — to private companies, with the notable exception of Stockton. Typically, the community owns the wells, the water-supplying lakes and ponds, or the water rights (in the West), and sends that water to the private company for treatment and delivery. While that arrangement has led to considerable controversy (in Atlanta, Lexington, and elsewhere), it is much better than allowing the water supply to be owned and controlled by the private company; in that case it is feared that the private company could use its ownership of the water supply as a bargaining chip in future contract negotiations (most contracts are for less than twenty years).[10]

Indianapolis is a good example of an instance in which a private company has controlled the water delivery systems — not the water supplies — efficiently and without price gouging, although not without problems.[11] The key to the success in Indianapolis is a carefully worded contract that lists in detail the binding expectations of the city. This has caused Veolia Water to adhere closely to the contract, in recognition that any violation may result in termination. This recognition is reflected in Veolia's promise to consumers:

> The Consolidated City of Indianapolis Department of Waterworks and Veolia Water North America Operating Services, Inc. are committed to continuous improvement in the provision of services to water customers. This commitment is shown by the nearly $10 million pay at risk annually based on Veolia Water's performance in key areas. Exhibit 12 of the Management Agreement between Veolia Water North America Operating Services, Inc. and the City of Indianapolis outlines the 40 incentive criteria. The incentive criteria address key areas including responsiveness to customer inquiries, delivery of quality water, success in controlling costs, and effectiveness in managing assets.[12]

Veolia acknowledges that success depends on a commitment from the city and the private water company — and that service comes before profits, which suggests that the company is committed to providing water at any cost. However, a lawsuit has been filed by citizens of Indianapolis against Veolia, charging that the opposite is occurring.[13] At this time that lawsuit has not yet been heard.

In still other instances, public officials have become concerned about losing control of the water utility (or at least a portion of it) but the general public has not. The optimal scenario is for water consumers (citizens) to notice no difference. As Angela Woodall stated, only when boil orders became more frequent did she become concerned. The bottom line for citizen satisfaction seems to be safe, healthy water delivered at minimal cost. In Atlanta and Stockton, that bottom line was breached, the private companies lost their contracts, and the management and operation of water delivery returned to the cities' water utility departments.

The concerns about for-profit companies are valid ones. There is simply no reason a city water utility should not be able to operate and manage a water delivery system as efficiently as a for-profit company. It appears to those opposed to privatization that city officials have punted the problems to a private company — and are more than willing to let the private company take the heat for raising rates. If old and obsolete water systems are in need of upgrades, the rates will need to be increased to meet the additional costs, whether a city or a private company is upgrading the system. Consumers will have to pay more, but by keeping the water delivery system in public ownership, they ensure that access to water won't be held hostage by a profit-driven private company.

In May 2006, I had a conversation with a high-ranking official of a private water company who said the following:[14]

> The things we look for are fairly simple. We want a water delivery system that is having problems — you know, old pipes, rusty water from those old pipes, a few boil orders, that sort of thing. We do not want a really old system where the only thing that can be done is to replace the whole thing. That costs way too much.
>
> Atlanta was a failure because there were many more problems than the City folks had told about. On one hand, maybe they knew and weren't forthright because they wanted a private company to take the blame. On the other hand, maybe they didn't know the extent of the problems but wanted someone else to bring the system up to speed. Whatever

the case — and there're arguments on both sides — Atlanta is not a good example to use for what happens when a private company takes over what had been a public system. I guess if you want to point to a failure, that's it.

But there are success stories all over the country — places where private companies have succeeded in doing what the public utilities couldn't or wouldn't do. One of the biggest and longest successes has been in Indianapolis — that's what we point to when we want to extol the virtues of a private-public partnership.

It works best when it is a private-public partnership and that arrangement is spelled out in the contract. In Atlanta, the company there took on too many responsibilities — ones they couldn't live up to. So the City had no choice. They had to terminate the contract — they had to take it back. No one really won: the city lost, the water company lost, consumers lost. Hell, everybody lost . . . and now Atlanta is stuck with the same problems it had before. The only difference is that the City will have to shoulder the entire load and rates will skyrocket with all the repairs, upgrades, and maintenance. Those things *must* be done, otherwise the water system will just totally fail. If it all falls apart, boil orders will be viewed as a good thing — at least it means there'll be water to boil. . . .

I've kind of gone around the bush, and each city or town that's looking to a private company to take over the water system is different. So what the water company is looking at may be a bit different each time. But there are some things that make an investment profitable — and like it or not, it is profit that motivates the private company. If it doesn't look as if the deal will turn a profit, the water company won't be interested.

In subsequent email interviews, this official laid out some of the considerations that private companies have before embarking on a project:

The water system needs some work, but not to the point that total replacement is called for.

The water system is old, but not too old. Atlanta's system is very old — some of it goes back to the early nineteenth century — and in that sense it was fairly stupid for any water company to try to bring it up to speed. On the other hand, fairly new systems don't need much — maybe not any — work, and so the owner of that system isn't even interested in turning it over. Without casting too much blame, the private company down in Atlanta should have looked over the problems — they shouldn't have taken the City's word for it, but should have done their own assessment. Instead, they went into it kind of blind and ended up with nothing.

The majority of citizens have to be persuaded that the City is cutting a good deal in turning to a private company. That was the problem out in Stockton — the majority of citizens became convinced that the City Council was trying to hide something, and the citizens rose up. Even in that situation, though, the deal between the City and the Water Company would have stood up and sooner or later, the deal would have been more or less accepted. What happened was that a savvy citizens' group took it to court and the judge found some things wrong and threw out the whole thing.

The City has to play a role. Indianapolis is a good example of that. There's a private company in charge of the water delivery system, but it is clear that the City is ultimately responsible. That's a good arrangement, and one that's appreciated by everybody involved. The City got rid of a liability, the water company is making money, and the citizens get good water and lots of it.

"But," the official concluded in one email, "Let's not kid ourselves. What the water companies — and that includes mine — see is a steady source of money. Everyone needs water. They drink it, cook with it, wash dishes in it, take a bath, make coffee...you name it, and it takes water. Water companies aren't stupid — they saw that literally every place people live is hooked up to the water system. What better guarantee of a long-term day-after-day moneymaker than being paid by a city to run their water system?"

By stating the simple reality of any for-profit endeavor, the water official essentially confirmed the fears of Public Citizen and other entities and thus gives further validity to their arguments that water utilities are too valuable a public asset for a city council to turn over to a private company. Water, they assert, is a public right and one that should not be subject to potentially unscrupulous, or at least single-minded, market forces.

The Myths and Realities of Privatization

Given all this controversy, private water companies have retorted that opponents of privatization have used misinformation to arouse an otherwise uninterested public. Veolia Water, the Indianapolis company, called these bits of information "myths" and responded on its Web page. There are similar claims on other Web pages, including those of OMI/Thames and *Reason* magazine. The public entities' responses to these "myths," below, are garnered from various sources, including individuals such as Vandana Shiva (an Indian economist and sustainable-use activist).[15] The "reality" is my take.

> **MYTH:** *A private company will own our water.*
>
> **Water company response:** In a public-private partnership, the public maintains ownership of all assets — and sets rates.
>
> **Public entities' response:** While it is true that ownership remains with the public, the day-to-day management and operation (including statements and bills) of a water utility will be in the hands of a for-profit entity.
>
> **Reality:** The day-to-day management and operations are what is important in this scenario.
>
> **MYTH:** *A private company will set our rates.*
>
> **Water company response:** Rate-setting authority remains the responsibility of the municipal customer. A partnership is not like a regulated utility in which a private-sector company owns assets and seeks rate increases. A public-private partnership is *not* privatization.
>
> **Public entities' response:** In reality, the water company will make a recommendation about rates to the city council,

which then seeks a rate increase (rates always go up, never down) from the public service commission (or other state agency that acts on requests for rate increases).

Reality: The key to this is the language in the contract. Reality dictates that if a private company recommends a rate increase, it is almost certain that city officials will go along with that and will seek to have that increase approved by a state commission. It should be further noted that in many states, the city response is the final response — no state approval is necessary.

MYTH: A private company will only drive costs up — so it can make a profit!

Water company response: There are now more than 2,000 North American communities served by public-private partnerships.[16] In the overwhelming majority of cases, costs decreased by 10 to 40 percent. For instance, Oklahoma City has saved more than $150 million through a partnership. A private-sector company's fee is based on a contractual agreement that is typically only adjusted upward in conjunction with increases in the consumer price index. The best testament to the stability of costs and the provision of good-quality water and service is the fact that only 2 percent of all partnerships reverted to municipal management in 2002, according to extensive research reported in the *Public Works Financing* newsletter.

Public entities' response: The myth should be about rates, not costs. Rates have never gone down, and most have gone up.[17] The company makes a profit by lowering costs and increasing rates.

Reality: While there is some truth to the assertion of the private water companies that cities that have adopted privatization have incurred lower costs, the fact is that consumers' rates have increased. Water companies prefer to talk about costs; public entities cite rates.

MYTH: *Privatization will cost municipal employees their jobs.*

Water company response: In most public-private partnerships, employees are terminated only for cause. Staff reductions are generally achieved by transfers or attrition.

Public entities' response: The water company usually employs municipal employees, meaning that public employees become employed by the private company. While there is some protection for employees provided by contracts, at issue are wage rates, pension funds, and other employee-employer issues. In most instances, benefits are transferred, but in other situations the employee must start over.

Reality: Again the contract is the key. It is not termination that is the problem, it is the number of employees. If positions are not filled when someone resigns or retires, then the number of employees goes down and the private company saves money.

MYTH: *Environmental compliance will erode.*

Water company response: Private-sector companies are often hired specifically to address a municipality's compliance issues.

Public entities' response: Many complaints have been filed against private for-profit companies in their operations of what once was a public utility. While private companies are often "hired to address a municipality's compliance issues," there is evidence that compliance problems become worse, not better, as is the allegation in the lawsuit against Veolia.

Reality: The Safe Drinking Water Act specifies the maximum contaminant level of various compounds, and neither the city nor a private company may exceed those. Compliance with standards is not at issue in privatization; rather, it is the cost to the city of infrastructure upgrades and commensurate rate increases.

MYTH: Companies pad the bottom line by cutting costs and laying off employees.

Water company response: Cities give their preferences regarding employees. And companies want to take advantage of employees' local knowledge.

Public entities' response: There is absolutely no doubt that private companies cut costs in order to show a profit, and there is documentation that one way this is done is by reducing the number of employees (for instance, by not replacing retiring workers).

Reality: There is no validity to the claim that private companies lay off employees. As noted above, there is validity to the claim that the total number of employees will be reduced through what is known as "natural attrition" — meaning that when an employee resigns or retires, the position is not filled.

MYTH: When given the opportunity, municipal employees prove the most efficient.

Water company response: Employee groups cannot provide financial guarantees. They cannot assume liabilities for operations and performance. They cannot finance the significant capital investments required by many projects.

Nor do employee groups have the experience that comes from adopting a wide range of technologies and management approaches in numerous conditions and settings.

Public entities' response: Municipal employees typically are unionized through the American Federation of County, State, and Municipal Employees (AFSCME). Water companies usually oppose such collective bargaining arrangements and are notoriously antiunion.

Reality: Water companies are not unionized and typically oppose collective bargaining efforts.

MYTH: Companies care only about profit, so the public should manage public resources.

Water company response: Private-sector profit does not come at the public's expense. Typical savings for municipalities range from 10 to 40 percent. Furthermore, partnerships enable more local control and flexibility to meet the community's needs.

Public entities' response: This gets at the central question: Is water a need or a right? If water is a right, there is no justification for a private company to extend this right and to make a profit from it. Private companies, in fact, cannot extend a right; only a governmental entity (a public entity) can do that.

Reality: Water for essential needs (drinking, cooking, bathing, washing clothes and dishes) should be considered a basic right, and one that only a government can extend. Private companies can offer privileges, not rights.

MYTH: The city will be left with a bucket of bolts.

Water company response: Contracts can easily be written so that assets are maintained and preserved. The municipal customer checks to ensure the proper functioning of assets. Finally, the public-sector customer always controls spending to help preserve the life of assets.

Public entities' response: In cities such as Atlanta, and cities in India and Chile, where contracts have been nullified by city councils or mayors, the infrastructure was left in arguably worse condition than before the private company was involved.

Reality: In cities where contracts have been voided, various infrastructure repairs and upgrades were left unfinished. In cities where contracts are in place, repairs and upgrades are being made, so it is suspected that the system will be in better shape.

MYTH: A new company just won't understand our system the way we do.

Water company response: Companies specializing in water are the same companies that drive innovation in the water industry's technology and operations. Municipal employees are readily welcomed into the private-sector family, as their local, public experience is blended with private-sector expertise. The majority of water company employees are former public-sector employees who are local to their communities.

Public entities' response: It is interesting that the water companies address only the issues pertaining to employment, and not to any issue involving citizen consumers. That is the critical failing in all water privatization schemes — the deals are cut behind closed doors — and only when negotiations are complete and a contract is signed are citizens allowed to view what was done in their name. In those instances where citizens' groups have become involved, those contracts have been broken mostly because various local concerns were *not* addressed.

Reality: Certainly, local consumers understand local problems better than a company headquartered in Europe.

Although companies operating out of France, England, or Germany adopt names that would lead one to believe that they're born in the USA, foreign ownership of water companies has been an ugly issue in a few areas. It is undeniably true that the major water companies — Suez, Vivendi, RWE Thames Water, even Veolia — are European companies. American Water, for example, was recently acquired by RWE, a German company. That ownership became an issue in Lexington, Kentucky, which was served by a subsidiary of American Water taken over by RWE — which placed American Water on the block.[18] Urban County, in which Lexington is located, proposed a buy-out, through eminent domain, of the Kentucky American Water company. RWE responded by stating that Kentucky American was not for sale — only the parent company, American Water, was. As of this writing, the matter is in court. While RWE filed a motion to dismiss the case, the judge did not agree. A number of citizens in Lexington with long memories don't like a previous enemy country owning their water system.

There are federal standards for drinking water. What comes out of the tap is carefully monitored to ensure that there are minimal levels of contamination. The key word is *minimal* — in the arcane language of Washington, D.C., and the Environmental Protection Agency, drinking-water purity must be within "maximum contaminant levels." This means that drinking water does contain various nasty things, but those have to be kept within certain limits. Those limits are based on the tolerances of healthy white males between the ages of nineteen and thirty-five.

It was not the purity of the water at issue in Mexico City, but rather the quantity. The concern that water companies will charge more with diminishing supplies gets at the essence of the issue: *Is access to clean drinking water a right — one held in common by all citizens?* If so, then privatization cannot occur because private companies don't deal in rights, but in privileges. If water is a *need*, then water companies are free to make a profit from providing clean drinking water to all. It is a subtle difference — a right or a need — but it makes a world of difference to thirsty people. The words of Vandana Shiva ring true: "Water can be used but not owned. People have a right to life and the resources that sustain it, such as water. The necessity of water to life is why, under customary laws, the right to water has been accepted as a natural, social fact. That is why governments and corporations cannot justify denying people their water rights. Water rights come from nature and creation. They flow from the laws of nature, not from the rules of the market."

[WHAT YOU CAN DO]

In Stockton, California, a small band of citizens questioned the turnover of a public water system to a private for-profit company. That small band grew to a majority of the citizens of that town and led to a successful challenge in court. Without those first few vocal citizens, the contract negotiated between a few public officials and water company employees would have gone unnoticed. A court of law ruled in favor of the citizens, and the water utility of Stockton reverted to public usage. One of the critical points in the court decision was that the decision to go with a private company was made, and then an environmental assessment was conducted. The judge pointed out that an assessment should not be done after the fact to justify a decision, but beforehand to help guide the decision. As far as the citizenry was concerned, pure, clean water — and lots of it — is a right that should not be placed in the hands of a private company. In Stockton, the private company was sent packing, and all has returned to normal: the water system is in public hands, is showing a profit, and is meeting state and federal compliance standards.

The key to access to water, then, is vigilance. While most local elected officials have nothing but the welfare of their constituents in mind, quite often contracts are negotiated and signed without any recognition of long-term community interests. The elected officials listen only to the enticements of private companies and do little in the way of fact-checking, nor do they review the record of the private company. It is imperative that citizens remain vigilant and be prepared to ask hard questions about the rights and needs of the consumers. There is nothing inherently wrong with the privatization of water as long as water is delivered in a manner that complies with all federal Safe Drinking Water Act standards, is delivered in sufficient quantity, and is delivered at low rates. The key question for citizens to ask is: Why is it that a private for-profit company can do this, but our town can't?

As noted above, water to meet essential needs should be a right, and only a government can extend a right. Water that is used for profit making is another matter, and that use can reasonably be considered a privilege. As noted, the United Nations has deemed that 50 liters per day is sufficient to meet human needs; anything above that should be considered a privilege. Unfortunately, at present, all consumers are charged the same rate. Privatization will not change that: it is to the advantage of the private company to assess a "one size fits all" rate. However, if water delivery systems are in public ownership, differential rates could be charged (the more water used above the 50-liter minimum, the higher the rate).

While national organizations — including the Sierra Club, Private Citizen, the Natural Resources Defense Council, the Public Interest Research Group — are excellent sources for information, brochures, posters, and other handouts, in the cities where privatization has been an issue, local groups have been the key to leading opposition and to eventually causing the private entity to go away. It is thus critical that citizens keep up with issues involving privatization by becoming attuned to city council hearings and deliberations and becoming involved in any attempt to turn the water supply or delivery over to a private company. Make sure that any contract with a private company contains clauses about service, rates, and employee benefits and numbers. As Margaret Mead once said, "Never doubt that a small group of thoughtful, committed citizens can change the world. Indeed, it is the only thing that ever has."

six

GLOBAL WARMING

The Wild Card That Could Leave
Us Flooded or Parched

In 1998, Jim and Evonna Wilson[1] learned of the proposed activities of a lead-mining company in their area. Concerned that the mining company's activities would foul their drinking water, they had the water from their springs tested so they would have some before-and-after data. The samples came back from the state health agency as suitable for drinking: the water from the springs met all the rigid tests for potable water and contained no contaminants. However, the tests proved unnecessary, because after considerable local opposition, the lead-mining company went away to try to find a more unsuspecting populace to locate next to. The Wilsons breathed a sigh of relief that their water supply would be unharmed. Then came an unprecedented five-year drought, and their springs completely dried up. Never in the recollection of old-timers had the springs stopped flowing. They had ebbed at times, but complete cessation was unheard of.[2]

Situations like these are occurring all over the country — and all over the world. The majority of the world's scientists are sounding the alarm about the increasing severity of storms, the longer-lasting droughts, and the overall increase in Earth's temperature — circumstances that many believe are directly related to global warming.[3] According to scientists at the National Center for Atmospheric Research, "Rising global temperatures appear to be a major factor [in drought]."[4]

So did the Wilsons' springs dry up due to a drought spurred by global warming? There's no way to know for sure, just as there is no way to state with certainty that Hurricane Katrina, which led to the evacuation of New Orleans, was caused or intensified by global warming. However, leading scientists agree that the temperature of the entire planet is steadily and dangerously increasing, and that it's disrupting our weather patterns. Although it's impossible to predict the exact specifics of how much the temperature will rise, or when and where, we know for sure that these changes in climate are intricately related to our planet's surface water resources.

The Latest Scientific Predictions

The Intergovernmental Panel on Climate Change (IPCC), whose members are appointed by the United Nations, is composed of the leading climatological scientists in the world. The IPCC was established in 1988 in response to reports from scientists around the planet that something was happening. Its specific charge is to "assess scientific, technical and socioeconomic information relevant for the understanding of climate change, its potential impacts and options for adaptation and mitigation."[5] In its most recent report, the IPCC makes several matters quite clear:

1. Global warming (usually labeled "climate change") is mostly anthropocentric (human caused) and is the result of the "burning of fossil fuels and changes in land cover."[6]

2. Flora and fauna that have adapted to current climate conditions in their ecosystems will fail to thrive — and some may become extinct.

3. There will be enormous social and economic upheaval in human communities.

4. Chaos will likely reign in political systems.

5. Sea levels will rise and coastal cities will be inundated.

These dire predictions are based on the assumption that actions will not be taken in time to prevent the worst effects of global warming. Of course, this needn't be the case if we take steps to make some key radical changes. But even though the scientific evidence is clear that we're headed toward a global crisis in the very near future, it's not easy to get people to change their habits — even if not doing so could mean the end of human civilization.

Humans don't react very well to incremental changes. This phenomenon is known to social scientists: human societies perform very poorly at preventing disasters, but we react fairly well to crises.[7] In the movie *An Inconvenient Truth*, Al Gore uses a cartoon frog to demonstrate this: If a frog is dropped into hot water, it will immediately leap out. But if it is placed in tepid water that is slowly heated to a boil, the frog will remain there until it is cooked. This scenario is strikingly similar to the way that the human race is failing to react to the slowly heating temperatures of our planet.

By the time the impacts of global warming reach the crisis stage — if we let it get to that point — humans will be reacting to worst-case scenarios. The drawback to waiting until a crisis occurs is that the upper atmosphere reacts very slowly to changes. What is up there will remain up there for decades. It took a long, long time for human activities to enhance the greenhouse gas effect, causing Earth's temperature to rise. The advent of the Industrial Age was in the late 1700s; only in 1988 were symptoms of global warming recognized. Once the tipping point has been reached — causing what scientists call a positive feedback effect — it will likely take centuries of reduced emissions for Earth's climate to return to "normal." Some assert that the climate change is permanent and that future conditions, even assuming a reduction in greenhouse gases, will in no way resemble today's. In short, by the time a crisis occurs, it will be too late to do anything about it. Like Al Gore's frog, we'll be cooked.

From the Greenhouse Effect to Global Warming

The greenhouse effect is the earth's natural climate-regulation process, which, when left unaltered by polluting modern technologies, keeps us from freezing or boiling. The way it works is that various gases (primarily carbon dioxide) in the earth's upper atmosphere let sunlight through but keep the generated heat in. The more gases in the upper atmosphere, the warmer things become. It is thanks to the greenhouse effect that our planet's temperature has been generally conducive to life as we know it. But human activities have emitted excessive gases into the upper atmosphere, which is increasing the amount of heat trapped in the atmosphere, thus increasing temperatures on the planet. From a life-giving greenhouse gas effect to a potentially life-threatening global warming, what is being experienced and forecast is too much of an otherwise good thing.

Carbon dioxide is the main greenhouse gas. In the natural world, a helpful amount of carbon dioxide is produced by animals breathing in oxygen and exhaling carbon dioxide. But some modern human activities have led to a steep increase of carbon dioxide in our atmosphere. Burning fossil fuels at coal-burning power plants and in each of the millions of cars we drive has become a main producer of carbon dioxide. Another significant source of carbon dioxide (and methane) is cow flatulence, a by-product of our extensive meat industry. Human activities and industry have added millions of tons of carbon dioxide gas to the earth's paper-thin upper atmosphere.

This increase in carbon dioxide production has been severely compounded by the destruction of millions of acres of forests (which retained carbon dioxide and acted as a sink, a storage container that could keep the amounts of carbon dioxide released into our atmosphere in check). When carbon dioxide is emitted though the burning of fossil fuels and has no place to go but up, the stage is set for catastrophic warming.

There are those who assert that forests now cover more acres in the United States than they did in 1600.[8] That is true in the grossest of senses, depending on how "forests" are defined. Many of today's forests consist of shrubs, brush, and saplings,[9] which don't provide the carbon sink that mature trees do. And chances are that, due to today's timbering techniques, those small trees will never reach maturity.[10] Moreover, the destruction of rain forests in Central and South America, and in Southeast Asia, greatly reduces the capture of carbon dioxide in those forests and sends this greenhouse gas up into the atmosphere.[11]

In addition to forest cover, the oceans of the world absorb much heat and act as a heat sink. At some point in the temperature creep, the oceans will become warm on the surface and no longer serve that function. At that point, global warming will leap from a peripheral concern to an enormous and immediate worldwide crisis — no more gradual changes, but a very abrupt one. Sea levels will rise dramatically from melting ice in the Arctic and Antarctic, inundating coastal cities. Some now-pleasant areas of the planet will become uninhabitable (some from heat and humidity, and some from heat and aridity). Agricultural crops will wither and die, and farmers will suffer financially or perish. The IPCC report concludes that anything humans do to upset the delicate balance of Earth's climate will inevitably result in changes that harm or destroy our way of life, including significant variations in temperature, precipitation, and the intensity of storms and other weather events.[12]

By the calculations of most climatologists, the average temperature of the entire planet has risen by about 1 degree in the last hundred years.[13] While that may not sound like much, it must be remembered that this is an average: In some spots, the rise has been much more dramatic. In other spots, no rise in temperature has been recorded. In still other areas, the average temperature has declined because of increased rainfall and cloud cover. There have been a number of speculations that global warming could result in another ice age in Europe if the Gulf Stream, which transports warm water and warm temperatures to the North Atlantic, ceases to exist. Ocean currents essentially act as a conveyor belt, carrying warm water to otherwise cold areas, and vice versa. If these currents are altered or cease altogether, the planetary climate would be immediately and dramatically altered. This is what is predicted to happen if the cold water in northern areas becomes warm.[14] The waters in the oceans have become warmer, which has led to an increasing number of hurricanes (because tropical depressions form over warm waters) with increasing strength. The warmer the water, the more intense the hurricane, which is one reason cyclonic storms lose strength over land masses. In 2005, the number of named storms (storms with a sustained wind velocity of over 45 mph) exhausted the letters of the English alphabet, and the last few had designations derived from the Greek.

In areas that could have the greatest impact on the rise of sea levels, the temperature is rising at unprecedented rates. In Alaska, for instance, the tundra is melting as temperatures have risen from 4 to 7 degrees in the past fifty years.[15] Low temperatures in this area are a bit higher, high temperatures are setting records, and winter is shorter and summer is longer. In these areas, there's no need for scientific studies to show that things are changing dramatically — all it takes is a bit of observation. Homes, roads, and pipelines built on once-frozen ground are shifting and sinking; the Arctic sea ice is melting about three weeks earlier than it did only thirty years ago, and polar bear populations are declining. Polar bears hunt seals through the sea ice for survival. When the ice disappears, so do the polar bears.

Glaciers worldwide are melting — when Glacier National Park was established in Montana in 1910, there were 150 glaciers. There are now 30, and these are much smaller and shrinking.[16] Glaciers form the headwaters for many western rivers and streams — if the glaciers melt, the upper reaches of the streams and rivers will cease to exist, and even downstream will see a diminishment of water

The pressing realities of global warming were recently and inadvertently confirmed by, of all entities, the Ventria Rice Company. Ventria Rice had proposed to raise its genetically modified crops in Missouri's Bootheel, a traditional rice-growing area due to a relatively warm climate, level fields, and fertile soils. However, there was a fear by traditional rice farmers that their crops would be contaminated, and Anheuser-Busch — the St. Louis beer maker that has a lot of clout in Missouri and is the world's largest buyer of rice — stated that it would stop buying rice from the Bootheel if Ventria were allowed to plant genetically modified crops. Ventria abandoned its plans for that area but proceeded to find a home in northeastern Missouri in the floodplains of the Missouri River. The land is level, the soil fertile. Rice is not grown in northeastern Missouri — the winters are too long and cold and the summers are short. But Ventria Rice is assuming that the climate will warm and the area will be friendly to the crop.[17] This assumption is based on predictions that global warming will make northern Missouri wetter and warmer. Ventria Rice is willing to take a huge financial gamble on the hope that we will do nothing as a nation or as a global community to address climate change and the human activities that are causing it.

How Global Warming Could Affect Our Water Supply

There are various forecasts regarding the availability of surface water, which includes both ocean water and freshwater. (Groundwater is not even mentioned in the IPCC report. While it is likely that groundwater stored in underground aquifers will not be directly affected by global warming, it's safe to assume that aquifers will continue to decline at current or even accelerated rates as surface water is no longer available.)[18] In order to understand why there is no consensus about how global warming will affect our surface waters, it's helpful to understand how the impacts of global warming itself are calculated.

There are more than five hundred thousand variables in global warming calculations for specific areas — and the impact of each variable must also be calculated.[19] That is why climatologists' predictions must be based on only a few hundred thermometer readings and the historical record; they believe that global warming is occurring, but how a specific area will be affected is essentially unknown. However, most of the five hundred thousand variables are not critical, and many can be discarded. The critical variables that remain create a more manageable, though possibly inaccurate, calculation. That is why many global warming reports on a specific area include the words "as far as is known" and "further study is warranted."[20]

This uncertainty about the effects of global warming on specific areas has led global-warming skeptics to call the entirety of the issue into question. It is crucial to understand that the overall circumstances of global warming are well established — leading climatologists unequivocally agree that global warming is occurring, even if they aren't exactly sure of when and where we will see its impacts. While some skeptics have been confused by this, others have been misinformed by the "findings" of scientists in the pay of the fossil fuel industry (oil, gas, coal). These industries, knowing full well that their products are having a disastrous impact on the planet, have given large infusions of cash to any scientists who publicize findings that distract from the impacts of their products.

Furthering the confusion, the press has given equal attention to these scientists for hire, which gives the general public and some of our top government officials the mistaken impression that there is genuine debate in the scientific community about the realities of global warming. Unfortunately for the fossil fuel industry, global warming is real. Scientific theories are based on facts, and while various pro and con articles have appeared in the popular press, the official jury is not out.[21]

Some might wonder what the benefit is of heeding scientific predictions that aren't guaranteed. To those who would rather wait until there is no uncertainty around this issue, I offer a quote from ecologists Paul and Anne Ehrlich: "If, when you leave your house, you know that the chances of a collision are 50 percent, wouldn't you fasten your seat belt?"[22] When your own personal life, or the life of all humankind, is at real risk, it makes sense to err on the side of caution and take predictions as warnings.

Keeping that in mind, let's review some of the region-specific predictions being made by top scientists about global warming. One such prediction, reflected somewhat by recent trends, is that the desert southwest — Arizona, New Mexico, southern California — will become wetter, with about 25 percent more precipitation.[23] This area will also become hotter.[24] Average daytime summer temperatures in Phoenix average about 104 degrees, so the area is used to a dry heat. But if the average daytime summer temperature[25] soars to 110 and the humidity goes up from the summer afternoon average of about

22 percent[26] to over 50 percent or even 70 percent, swamp coolers (which are dependent on evaporation, which is in turn dependent on low humidity) will no longer function. One minor, seemingly trivial, consequence, then, of global warming is that air conditioners would become a necessity for Phoenix residents. Obviously, those on low or fixed incomes would be unable to afford them. Low-income folks — and there are many in Phoenix — would either perish from the heat or be forced to move to more hospitable areas.

Even though the computer models used by climatologists are only as accurate as the inputted data allow, climatological predictive maps do agree on some points, with cautionary statements.[27] It is likely that the central Midwest — Missouri, Iowa, Illinois — will become wetter and even cooler, with a relatively stable climate (no extremes of hot and cold). This prediction is based on a scenario in which an almost-constant cloud cover would generate much rain and, at the same time, keep temperatures cooler. The result of an enhanced greenhouse gas effect in the central Midwest might well be the opposite of what might be expected from global warming.[28] The High Plains, by contrast, are likely to become much hotter and even more arid. While this is already a land of little rain, global warming is likely to make precipitation even skimpier. From Nebraska to New Mexico (west of the 100th meridian, which runs through the Dakotas, Nebraska, Kansas, Oklahoma, and Texas) rainfall averages about 15 inches per year.[29] That average is expected to fall to less than 10 inches (which means that in some years there would be less than 10 inches and in other years, more). In the area west of the 100th meridian and defined by northeast New Mexico, southeast Colorado, southwest Kansas, and northwest Oklahoma, the precipitation could well be zero. An average is just that, an average: some years less, and others more.

Likewise, the Texas Panhandle will be hot and dry.[30] All

of this bodes ill for the massive Ogallala Aquifer, currently declining — mostly due to agricultural irrigation — by about 24 inches per year. With the increased aridity, farmers will depend even more on irrigation, and the only place to get water is from the Ogallala.

At the other extreme is Florida, which can expect an excess of water — albeit salty water. While temperatures are expected to rise in this area, the increased precipitation and the rising sea level are what will most heavily — and negatively — affect the Sunshine State.[31] Storms will become more numerous and severe as the waters in the gulf become warmer. Coastal cities — Miami, Tampa, St. Petersburg, Jacksonville — will be overwhelmed by the rising sea and may well become uninhabitable, if they're not destroyed by hurricanes first.[32]

The predictions on how San Francisco and Los Angeles will be affected by global warming vary widely, with some models predicting hot and wet,[33] and others hot and dry.[34] It is anticipated that the water sources of these cities will become more sporadic and undependable. Rising temperatures will mean that more precipitation in the Sierra and the southern Rockies will fall as rain, not snow.[35] Rain runs off quickly; snow melts and releases water slowly. It is likely, then, that access to water will be boom and bust as rivers flood in the winter and spring, then dry up in the summer and fall.[36] If global warming is left unchecked, there will be dramatic changes all over our country and the world. The Rio Grande and Colorado may become flush, or they may become dry. Los Angeles and San Francisco may become uninhabitable due to water shortages while brackish and undrinkable water runs through the streets and into homes and businesses. Assumptions that led to laws, contracts, compacts, and water rights agreements were based on circumstances that will no longer exist.

Global warming is the great wild card when it comes to the future of our surface water supply. Many of this country's largest and most important metropolitan areas — including Miami, New Orleans (which has already suffered from Hurricane Katrina), and Houston — are located in areas that could be subject to severe flooding and dramatic oceanic storms if there are even minuscule rises in sea levels. These rising sea levels, due to the melting of polar ice caps and the Greenland ice sheet, are predicted to occur by 2099.[37] If the sea level continues to rise at the current rate (although it might rise faster if warmer seas cannot absorb excess heat),[38] low-lying coastal cities are likely to be inundated. Those coastal cities harbor a large percentage of this country's population, and more than half the population lives within an hour of a coast.[39] It's impossible for us to fully imagine what will happen when residents of those coastal areas are forced to move inland, en masse. The fallout from Hurricane Katrina, as well as its impact on New Orleans, should be a wake-up call. These kinds of storms and the subsequent human suffering are only predicted to increase.

Instead we "keep on keeping on" — doing all the things that will inevitably lead to more, not less, global warming. For example, a number of the nation's mayors have signed on to the U.S. Mayor's Climate Protection Agreement (adopting most of the somewhat modest articles of the Kyoto Protocol, which all nations except the United States and Australia have signed), yet many of those same mayors are advocating more activities (such as coal-burning power plants) that raise Earth's temperature. In the Midwest, for example, the mayor of Kansas City, Kay Barnes, signed the U.S. Mayors Climate Protection Agreement but is pushing for a doubling of the Kansas City Power and Light's coal-burning power plant. Columbia, Missouri, signed on to the U.S. Mayors Climate Protection Agreement only after inking contracts with Kansas City Power and Light's proposed expansion and with a huge new coal-fired plant in southern Illinois (Peabody's Prairie State mine-mouth plant). According to Albert Einstein, this is the definition of insanity: doing the same thing over and over again and expecting different results.[40]

[WHAT YOU CAN DO]

Climate changes that are now incremental will at some point become a full-blown crisis if we don't take dramatic and immediate action. The longer we delay, the more dire will be the result.[41] The problem of global warming is indeed global in nature, and that's a bit overwhelming to most people, even the growing majority (currently 85 percent of U.S. citizens)[42] who acknowledge that global warming is real and that it's the major threat to life on our planet. According to the U.S. Bureau of the Census, this country uses 25 percent of the earth's resources, and the film featuring Al Gore — *An Inconvenient Truth* — states that the United States is responsible for fully one-third of global emissions of the greenhouse gas carbon dioxide. This means that as Americans, we can and must make the most dramatic and immediate changes.

While politicians of all stripes and parties dither and do nothing, for fear of annoying the influential fossil fuel industry, and seem reluctant to impose any mandatory actions (although they are quite keen on voluntary ones, which only seem to result in ever-rising emissions), it falls to individuals to do something.

Fortunately, there is much that individuals can do.

For one thing, the United States consumes an enormous amount of the world's energy.[43] For a second thing, the largest two sources of greenhouse gases — and the largest two causes of global warming — are automobile emissions[44] and the fossil fuels burned to create most of our nation's electricity.[45]

An estimated 628 million cars are on U.S. roads (or 2.1 cars per person),[46] resulting in 314 million tons[47] of carbon dioxide being added to our atmosphere every year or about 45 percent of the automotive emissions of the entire world.[48] In the words of George W. Bush, the American people are "addicted to oil."[49] We are, and this addiction has been abetted by the automobile industry, which has fought bitterly — claiming technical, manufacturing, and cost issues — any attempt to increase the fleet standards (also called CAFE, for Corporate Average Fuel Economy, standards).[50] The current fleet average (light trucks are not included in this) is about 27 miles per gallon. If this number were increased to even 30 mpg, there would be a commensurate reduction in emissions of carbon dioxide. We would still be the world leader in emissions, however, simply because of the number of automobiles we possess. This means that while these slight improvements in fuel efficiency would do a bit of good, it's only a small start to fixing the problem.

While consumer support for fuel-efficient cars has been weak, this is beginning to change as gasoline prices soar. A few years ago, in the era of cheap fuel, the vast majority of consumers barely paid attention to the gas mileage rating when considering a new or used vehicle. Not so anymore: fuel economy has become quite important. Purchases of gas-guzzling SUVs and light trucks have fallen drastically. Toyota and Honda, the manufacturers of high-mileage hybrid cars, report thriving sales figures,[51] while sales of large gas guzzlers have led to declining sales for General Motors.[52]

The better the gas mileage a car gets, the less its greenhouse gas emissions. So if you must rely on an automobile for transportation, one of the most helpful steps you can take is to purchase a vehicle that gets a high rating on fuel economy. The U.S. Environmental Protection Agency makes such estimates and places these right on the sales stickers, making such a consideration easy.[53] A number of organizations from Public Citizen to the Sierra Club have been advocating increasing the CAFE standard, but market forces in a time of high gasoline prices will push higher sales for cars with higher gas mileage ratings.

The second step is a bit more difficult, but not for those living in areas where the temperatures remain well above freezing even in winter. Don't use your car. Walk. Ride a bike. Take public transportation. It is easy to walk and bike in the summer even in northern cities. In areas where it is dangerous to do so, greater public demand will result in the appearance of bicycle lanes, and more pedestrian-friendly intersections will be designed. Taking public transportation is easy and cheap in most cities. Buses and light rail are readily available — and for the most part are subsidized by the local, state, and federal governments. In some large cities, such as New York, Washington, and San Francisco, cars are often viewed as a hindrance, as parking spaces are few and far between. Taking the bus, riding a bicycle, or walking will not only cost far less but will also ease the demand for oil and gas and will ultimately scale back global warming.

As we address the emissions brought about by fossil-fuel-dependent transportation, we must also simultaneously address how we generate our electricity. Coal-burning power plants release more than 40 percent of the total of carbon dioxide into the atmosphere.[54] Some of the other pollutants released are immediately harmful to human health: oxides of nitrogen (precursors of ozone, or smog), mercury, and sulfur. Mercury causes all sorts of disorders of the central nervous system, including damage to the brain.[55] Various compounds of sulfur cause acid rain, responsible for sterile lakes and dead trees on the East Coast. While these byproducts are surely toxic to humans and the environment, it is the more than 2 billion tons[56] of carbon dioxide that these U.S. power plants release into the atmosphere each year that intensify global warming. Burning coal — burning anything, for that matter — converts copious amounts of oxygen to carbon dioxide, the primary greenhouse gas. The more there is in the upper atmosphere, the warmer things become. Coal-burning power plants are the number one source for emissions of carbon dioxide,[57] exceeding even the automobile.

The emissions soar during daylight and early evening hours, and utility companies charge the highest rates and make their money on what are known as peak hours — times of heavy demand. If you reside in an area barely meeting its electrical demand, chances are that the utility company places occasional alerts on local media outlets, asking that heavy power users such as clothes dryers, dishwashers, and other appliances be used later in the evening. Peak hours begin just after 5 PM and last until about 7 PM in the hot days of summer. The local power folks — responsible for seeing to it that the light comes on when the switch is flicked — must plan around this demand. In doing so, they buy about 15 percent more electricity than is needed to meet that peak — that excess is a "reserve."[58] Most reserve capacity is supplied by coal or natural-gas-fired power plants. If the demand goes up in areas using all of their reserves, electricity, almost all of it produced by coal-burning power plants (with a sprinkling of turbines at dams and a few nuclear plants — each with its own set of problems) will not be provided. If on the other hand, conservation and efficiency efforts lead to a de-creased load, not as much electricity will be needed, much less will be supplied, and coal-burning plants won't emit nearly as much carbon dioxide or other noxious compounds.

The United States leads the world in the consumption of electricity.[59] However, a few simple steps can reduce your electric bill, reduce the demand for electricity, and reduce greenhouse gas emissions. Most of the steps are enumerated above, and I will not repeat them here except to note that all of these involve more a efficient use of appliances, including heating and cooling systems.[60] No sacrifices are necessary, no reduction in the quality of life. Just do as your father said and turn off the light when you leave a room. Turn off computers at night. Do the laundry or the dishes during nonpeak hours (not from 5 PM to 7 PM) — not just when the utility folks tell you to, but all the time.

Remember the Wilsons, the folks whose springs dried up?[61] Jim and Evonna are a prime example of how personal choices can result in great reductions in global warming gases. After retirement, they relocated from a crowded urban area to a backwoods location — one that did not have electricity. It was 7 miles to the nearest power line, and they made a choice to go off the grid by using solar power. It was far cheaper to use solar panels — even with the outlay for photovoltaic cells, storage batteries, and an inverter (12-volt to 120) — than to acquire easements and pay for 7 miles of cable and poles. Additionally,

Jim and Evonna figured, they'd never need to make a utility payment.

Their system does require a bit of oversight, but they do not live a deprived life. They have a big-screen TV and several computers and monitors. Jim has a separate photovoltaic system set up for his workshop, which includes a power saw and welder and a workout room. They have hot and cold running water, thanks to a photovoltaic array for their well and an on-demand water heater. A cellular telephone keeps them in contact with the outside world. Jim and Evonna are rightly proud that their system is pollution free. They are not contributing at all to the coming global crisis: their system uses non-carbon-emitting sunlight to provide all the energy they need or want.

Obviously, not everyone can shell out the dough for a photovoltaic system — the upfront expenses are daunting. But the point is that reducing electrical consumption does not mean that sacrifices must be made. All that needs to be done is change a few habits, and literally, the world will be changed. Similar changes need to be accomplished by commercial establishments — it is costly to leave the lights on all night or to keep the thermostat set at 72 degrees when no one is present.

What the Wilsons are doing is a small-scale version of using alternative energy — tapping into the sun and wind to generate electricity. From the mesas of Texas to the ridges in Wyoming and Montana, wind generators are providing nonpolluting power. While photovoltaic cells (they capture the sun's rays) are the choice for individuals, wind generation provides electricity for communities. While even the most optimistic predictions do not envision shutting down polluting power plants, up to 15 percent of this nation's electrical demand could be met through wind generation.[62] A switch to wind generation amounted to a reduction of 27 million tons of carbon dioxide in Europe.[63] Similar reductions are expected here, since the population of the United States is equivalent to that of Europe.

Reducing demand for electricity is ecologically and economically the right thing to do. So is reducing reliance on the automobile or pushing for higher CAFE standards. Will these steps stop global warming? Not if they are the only steps taken, but when they're combined with all the other actions that citizens can take, maybe the tipping point to disaster can be avoided, and maybe all those water compacts, contracts, and agreements will remain in force. Ultimately it may mean that people in Phoenix will still be able to live there with enough water to sustain them, the humidity won't rise to the point that their swamp coolers no longer work, and folks in Florida and the other coastal areas along the Atlantic, Pacific, and Gulf of Mexico won't be inundated by stronger and more frequent hurricanes.

seven

TECHNOLOGICAL SOLUTIONS

The Skyrocketing Cost of a Glass of Water

M any people believe that technology will save us from water shortages. In this chapter, we'll review some of the high-tech solutions under consideration — desalination plants, pipelines and aquifers, groundwater pumping, and towed icebergs and huge waterbags — and examine how viable they are.

Desalination: Desperate Times Call for Costly Solutions

This is a water planet. We have many vast oceans — the Pacific and Atlantic, to name but two — and indeed, more than 97 percent of this planet's water is seawater.[1] There is one significant problem, however, with water taken from these oceans. It is unpalatable.

Not only does the water taste bad, but it can also lead to serious illness and death.[2] Humans, other animals (except for a few marine mammals), and terrestrial plants cannot use salt water. Essentially, any water that contains salt in amounts above a thousand parts per million is deadly to people. Ironically, drinking water from the ocean does not quench thirst at all but has the opposite effect: the salt in seawater uses up more of the body's water supply than is consumed.[3]

While the salt and the other minerals in seawater do not allow us to drink it directly, we can convert it into potable water. The process is a fairly simple one and has been recognized for millennia. In fact, Mother Nature provides the example: Evaporation itself removes all the minerals from water. The water goes up, and the minerals stay behind. Sunshine on the surface of the world's oceans converts highly mineralized water into freshwater that falls as rain. It picks up various minerals, runs off into streams and rivers and thence into the ocean — where these minerals are concentrated to such a degree that the water becomes again undrinkable.[4]

The primary mineral, salt, can be removed in a process called desalination. There are two main types of desalination plants — reverse osmosis and distillation — and each has advantages and drawbacks. In reverse osmosis, salt water is pumped through a semipermeable membrane such as plastic or rubber, which strains out the salts and other contaminants. The quality of the water produced depends on how much force is applied to the water as it is pumped through the membrane, how pure the water is, and how clean and permeable the membrane is. The quality can be improved by pumping the water through a second membrane.[5]

Reverse osmosis results in a large volume of water, but it is inefficient and horrendously expensive. The water has to be pretreated to remove as many particles as possible, and the membrane has to be cleaned daily or more often. The resulting water also retains some salt, although well within drinking-water standards.

The other method of desalination is distillation. There are several methods of distillation, but the differences among them are not significant.[6] They all involve heating the seawater and then removing the dissolved minerals through condensation. Although distillation effectively removes all the minerals from seawater and produces higher-quality water than reverse osmosis, it requires a vast amount of energy (in the form of heat) to do so. Few desalination plants use distillation, mostly because of the somewhat low yield derived from an enormous amount of expended energy.

Given the massive amounts of water stored in the oceans, it is little wonder that clever engineers and entrepreneurs look out over the seas and see profits. So far, however, all the schemes have been thwarted because no one has yet invented a fast, cheap method to remove salt from seawater. When the sun shines on the 156 million square miles of the Pacific Ocean, evaporated water by the billions of acre-feet daily is contained in the storm clouds that reach the northwestern United States and western Canada. But humans don't work on such a scale. Desalination plants — whether they're reverse osmosis or distillation — are minuscule by comparison and are consequently capable of delivering only relatively minuscule amounts of water (the largest such reverse osmosis plant, in Saudi Arabia, produces 128 million gallons, or about 382 acre-feet, per day.) These plants are also quite costly, and the water produced is likewise costly — estimates range from $500 to $2,000 per acre-foot[7] (average rates for freshwater in the United States are less than $100 per acre-foot). Only the wealthiest towns, cities, and residents are able to afford such water.

The second problem with desalination is inefficiency. Due to the somewhat clumsy designs of desalination plants, only about 15 to 50 percent of the salt water becomes freshwater.[8] That percentage will likely improve as better designs come out, but the amount of freshwater produced will never equal the amount of seawater going in. Not even Mother Nature achieves a one-to-one ratio.

The third problem with mass desalination is that it involves disposing of the salt and other minerals removed in the process. If, for example, a desalination plant achieves 50 percent efficiency (that is, for each gallon of salt water, a half gallon of freshwater is produced), the remaining water contains the salt and other minerals. Considering that the freshwater output of desalination plants is measured in acre-feet (1 acre-foot is about 326,000 gallons), this is not a trivial problem, and it constitutes a major obstacle in any significantly sized desalination facility. Obviously, this leftover water cannot simply be dumped into the surrounding ocean: the dramatic increase in salinity caused by the solution (also known as brine) would be fatal to marine plant and animal species. Since desalination plants are generally located on oceans and near urban areas, it is difficult to transport the waste product to land and to properly contain it so that it does not leach into any surface or underground waters.[9]

High costs, inefficiency, and problems with waste disposal — these would seem to deter consideration of desalination plants as a solution. But water is a necessity of life, and people will go to great lengths to obtain it. Currently, there are more than twelve thousand desalination plants worldwide.[10] The vast majority of these plants are in the Middle East, where the combination of aridity and wealth from oil makes desalination both desirable and possible. To date, there are fewer than two thousand desalination plants in the United States — and most of these are small or experimental, even in thirsty and heavily populated California. At this time, no water supply and delivery entity in the state is considering desalination plants as a major source of drinking water, primarily because the cost of desalination is generally higher than the costs of other available alternatives (water transfers and groundwater pumping, for example). However, as drought conditions intensify and concern over water availability increases, desalination projects are being investigated at numerous locations.

The increasing need for water in the West has coincided with an advance in the field of reverse osmosis. Referred to as EDR (electrodialysis reversal),[11] this process has much promise for the drinking-water supplies of coastal cities. EDR takes reverse osmosis one step further, subjecting the membranes to an electric charge. The positive ions of water, which have previously been charged, pass through the membranes under pressure, and salts and other minerals are removed. Every fifteen minutes the polarity is reversed, and the process is repeated ad infinitum.[12] The big advantage of EDR, according to the company that developed this process (Ionics, a subsidiary of General Electric) is that the plant does not need to be shut down to remove the collected minerals from the membranes. Facilities can operate without pause. EDR is being considered by the City of San Diego, which sees desalination as at least a partial solution to its increasing water needs.

The City of San Diego recently authorized a study for the construction of a desalination plant to provide some portion (as yet undetermined, but perhaps 15 percent) of that city's water supply. The city council contracted with RBF Consulting to conduct this study, which will cost approximately $825,000, but grants from the State of California and the Environmental Protection Agency will pay for about two-thirds of the costs.[13] It is anticipated that the plant will be built on the site of the now-abandoned San Onofre nuclear power plant. While costs to build the plant will be the primary focus of the study, other problems have already been identified. The intake pipes will suck in far more water than did the nuclear power plant — which used the water for cooling purposes — and there is much concern that sea life will be killed in the process.[14] The plant is to eventually provide 80 million gallons per day of potable water to the residents of San Diego — although a lengthy study to address all the problems, including the possible environmental harm, and the lengthy construction period are expected to delay the opening of the plant to 2020.[15]

In addition to the potential environmental hazards of this plant, its construction also raises issues about privatizing elements of an area's water supply and delivery system. As discussed in chapter 5, citizens across the country and worldwide are already alarmed by intrusions of private companies into local water delivery systems. This issue is definitely one of contention in San Diego, since the San Onofre site is owned by Edison (the company has leased this site to the U.S. Navy through 2025). Ray Golden, spokesperson for Southern California Edison, neglected to mention the possible pitfalls (the costs of desalination, waste disposal, damage to sea life, upgrades to pumps) in his presentation to municipal officials.

Rather than acknowledge these potential problems, he chose to focus only on selling a positive outlook on the situation.[16]

Given that the EDR process is patented — even though it is just an advancement of an age-old system, it is considered a proprietary development — it could well be that Ionics will be either contracted to construct and operate the facility or will sell this technology to the San Diego County Water Authority.

Even if the environmental and privatization issues can be sufficiently resolved, it's unclear if the current EDR technology can support the plant. While EDR is fairly new technology that will no doubt develop, it has been tested on only 1.6 million gallons per day or less, not the 80 million deemed to be desirable by the San Diego Water Authority. Ionics touts a conversion rate of 85 percent from salty to fresh and also asserts that up to 94 percent of the "solids" from seawater can be removed, meaning that EDR is somewhere between reverse osmosis and distillation in terms of efficiency.

Because the population of the San Diego area is growing rapidly and attracting new water-heavy industry, the county's water authority has become a leader in finding innovative ways to convert seawater to fresh and potable water. All that water in the Pacific Ocean (on which San Diego is located) is viewed as a means of relieving the area's water woes. Currently, the authority is involved in investigating the feasibility of a reverse osmosis desalination plant at Carlsbad — in the northern part of the county.[17] This plant would use the more conventional technology — not EDR — and would be seen as an adjunct to the EDR facility in San Onofre. The plant would produce up to 50 million gallons per day using eleven reverse osmosis "trains."

While some of the waste from reverse osmosis is brine and can be redeposited in the ocean (although, as noted, there are significant problems with that), some of the waste is in solid form and must be transported to a landfill designed to prevent leaching to surface and ground waters. The volumes of seawater — about 100 million gallons per day — to be taken into the desalination facility is also of concern because such massive intakes may result in the destruction of oceanic life. It can readily be seen that the Carlsbad plant will not be terribly efficient: 100 million gallons of salty water must be taken in to produce 50 million gallons of water that meets drinking-water standards. The facility would also require huge amounts of electricity to operate the pumps that intake the water and create the necessary pressure for the reverse osmosis systems to work. While the draft environmental impact report downplays these problems — and proposes mostly inadequate solutions — these matters could well lead to abandonment of this project. If so, then it is likely that the EDR desalination facility would also be abandoned. If the proven (but costly) technology of reverse osmosis causes extreme harm and has a number of insurmountable problems, then the experimental technology of EDR would be difficult to promote. San Diego would be back to where it is now: looking for a new source of water.

However, its examination of these two desalination processes is indicative of the seriousness of the water shortages facing the San Diego County Water Authority. That such speculative solutions are being considered points out a harsh reality: Right now, more than 80 percent of the county's drinking water comes from outside the county — and those resources are bitterly contested by those upstream.[18] As of this writing, the San Diego County Water Authority is spending over a million dollars per year on a water conservation program, yet water supplies continue to dwindle as demand increases.[19]

It could well be said that San Diego is simply trying to develop solutions to an upcoming problem — and is therefore doing the right thing. The water authority is counting on EDR's panning out, as its official newsletter states: "Since more than

80 percent of the San Diego region's water is imported, the San Diego County Water Authority is diligently seeking ways to develop local water sources. Seawater desalination is a viable option for providing drought-proof, locally treated water to support the economy and quality of life for San Diegans. Having studied seawater desalination since 1992, the Water Authority identified this source in 2004 as the best new supply for San Diego County's future."[20]

Cities up and down the West Coast, from the Bay Area to Los Angeles County, are facing the same problem: too many thirsty people, too little water. Inland is little better. All major metropolitan areas in the southwestern United States face growing shortages of water and are struggling to find new sources — sources that may not exist. Rather than limit population growth and development in these areas (which explorer John Wesley Powell advised over a century ago should not be inhabited),[21] these counties and cities are pushing full speed ahead on growth and development, while their dependence on water is based on hope and new technologies. While "water buffaloes" (water rights' attorneys) may insist that the shortage of water will not prevent such growth and development,[22] reality dictates otherwise.

Desalination may well be the answer for coastal cities. Such is not the case for the inland cities of Sacramento, Las Vegas, or Phoenix. These cities lack access to seawater. They must find other sources or dry up.

Pipelines and Aqueducts: Old Ways, New Methods

There is nothing new about transporting water through pipes or aqueducts. The Roman Empire relied on those mechanisms. In fact, some historians assert that Rome's method of ensuring against leakage — using lead to join segments of the pipes and aqueducts — led to the downfall of the empire. There were, no doubt, other reasons, and that particular problem does not exist today — other, presumably nontoxic, compounds are used to join pipe and aqueduct sections.

The only difference between a pipe and an aqueduct is, at first glance, superficial: a pipe is a usually round and usually metallic enclosed structure. An aqueduct is normally built of leak-proof cement but is open to the air. Aqueducts, essentially cement-lined ditches, are easier to construct. Although both pipelines and aqueducts use pumps and gravity, aqueducts usually depend on gravity to move water; pipelines are more dependent on pumps. Pipelines, not being exposed to the surface, don't lose water to evaporation and are not subject to various contaminants from the open air (bird droppings, for example).

These old-modern technologies are used by most major cities throughout the country. New York brings its water from the Adirondacks through pipes.[23] Los Angeles uses both pipelines and aqueducts.[24] The Central Arizona Project transports water from the Colorado River to the high, dry, and hot portions of that state, and it uses both pipes and aqueducts.[25] Even Las Vegas relies on a pipeline to bring water from Lake Mead to that city's thirsty inhabitants and tourists.[26] While a few new pipelines are being proposed, there is nothing new about the concept. The aqueduct that brings water from the Colorado River to Los Angeles was completed in 1913, nearly a hundred years ago. The Central Arizona Project brought water to Phoenix in the 1970s. The pipelines to some eastern and midwestern cities have been in place as long as the cities have been there (New York began taking water from the Adirondacks in the 1700s). Such developments went almost unnoticed or were applauded by the residents of thirsty communities and by the farmers and ranchers who received large volumes of this life-giving substance.

Now, however, pipeline proposals generate much controversy — as can be attested to by the city leaders of St. George, Utah, at the center of a rapidly growing area in southwestern Utah. That area wants to build a pipeline to and extract water from Reservoir Powell.[27] This pipeline will be tremendously expensive, but that is not the reason Utah residents and many others are upset. It seems that the pipeline would cross through several national parks and what is now a de facto wilderness area. In addition, St. George would be taking water from a reservoir that was never designed to supply drinking water. As pointed out in chapter 1, Reservoir Powell is at its lowest level since it was first filled — and the concern is that the St. George pipeline would further lower the declining lake. At this time, many studies must be performed and many permits issued before this pipeline will be approved.

The St. George pipeline illustrates a significant problem with using pipelines and aqueducts as solutions to a water shortage: few remaining areas can be considered ample sources of freshwater. Most of the rivers — and their tributaries — in this country have long been dammed for flood control, irrigation, recreation, and water resources. The waters of such mighty rivers as the Missouri, Mississippi, Ohio, Rio Grande, and Colorado have been retained in massive reservoirs behind equally massive dams.[28] While many of these dams were built for other purposes, the waters behind those dams are being increasingly diverted for municipal uses — primarily for drinking water.

It will also become more common to purchase land as a way of owning the water rights related to that land. T. Boone Pickens may have been quite astute in 1997 when he bought up lands in north Texas and offered to sell water to Amarillo and Lubbock.[29] And as water rights are purchased in areas relatively devoid of people, pipelines and aqueducts will be necessary to move that water from where it is to where it is needed.

Costs will not come down — in fact, every prediction is that water will become more expensive. But in order to sustain the current levels of growth — spurring the need for more and more water — it is likely that the costs of water transportation will be met.

Las Vegas is an example of a city that has run out of water. The Colorado River Compact of 1922 never anticipated that Nevada would become the residence of so many people, and consequently, Nevada was allocated fewer acre-feet than any other state.[30] According the to U.S. Census, Las Vegas is now the fastest-growing city in this country, and it takes all of the Colorado River water to which it (and Nevada) are entitled. Since there is much reluctance by all states involved to reopen negotiations leading to a compact that reallocates Colorado River water, Las Vegas, Clark County, and water czarina Pat Mulroy have been forced to look elsewhere.

"Elsewhere" at this point seems to be the groundwater resources under the rural northeast areas of Nevada — particularly under White Pine County.[31] That county has rejected an offer of $12 million for seventy-five years of its water — but higher offers are certain to follow. Aside from the problems created by selling off a valuable resource, there are at least two overriding issues here: (1) White Pine County is a long way from Las Vegas's Clark County, and the only realistic way to get such water to Las Vegas is to construct an enormous pipeline, and (2) the water in question is underground and would need to be drilled and pumped (a high-tech solution that will also be discussed in this chapter).

Any pipeline from White Pine to Clark County would be extremely difficult to build and consequently would be costly. The pipeline would also have to traverse one of the world's great deserts. To build a pipeline through a hot and dry desert would cause loss of human life and wildlife and would cause the most capable engineering firm to blanch. But if an offer is made that White Pine County cannot refuse, the wells will be drilled, the groundwater will be pumped, and a pipeline will transport this costly water from White Pine to Clark County. At present, a network of 345 miles of pipeline is proposed. Part of the network is needed to get the water from the wells and into the main pipeline. To sweeten its offer, the Southern Nevada Water Authority, based in Las Vegas, has proposed diverting a small portion of the water (5,000 acre-feet out of a total of 91,000 acre-feet the first year, and for only the first year) to developing areas of White Pine County. Still, all of White Pine County's water will otherwise be taken by Las Vegas, and if Las Vegas continues to grow, its offer will provide only temporary relief.

As water crises intensify, the push to construct elaborate and costly pipelines and aqueducts will no doubt intensify as well. In 1981, a pipeline was proposed to transport water from the Missouri River to replenish the Ogallala Aquifer.[32] This pipeline — running from near Atchison to Olympia, Kansas — would have been more than 400 miles long and would not have served any community on the High Plains. Its sole purpose would have been to take water from the Missouri River to replenish a vast underground reservoir that is being rapidly depleted.

At the time, the notion was rejected by Congress — actually, not even considered — due to the high cost. But, because of the agricultural benefits provided by lands irrigated by the Ogallala Aquifer and its rapid depletion, the idea will no doubt be raised again. If the pipeline is ever built, it will be the largest and longest public construction project to essentially run water into the ground. There is sure to be opposition from the State of Missouri, which depends on a reliable and sustainable source of Missouri River water. It will all come down to a cost-benefit analysis (ideally, the monetary benefits would outweigh the costs), to lobbying efforts by those representing the interests of the High Plains, and to the influence of elected officials from the states supplied by the waters from the Ogallala Aquifer versus "downstreamers," who will question any cost-benefit analysis, mount their own lobbying efforts, and engage Missouri's elected officials. This is likely to be the ultimate water war within the United States and one that will be fought for many, many years. If agricultural irrigation continues at the present rate, the Ogallala will probably be completely dry by the time this issue is resolved.

Other pipeline and aqueduct issues loom throughout the United States, from the Garrison Diversion in North Dakota (which would take Missouri River water to Devils Lake) to Punta Gorda[33] and Charlotte County, Florida (where there is wrangling over water from the Peace River)[34] to Clifton Park, New York (involving water from the Hudson River).[35] The issues seem almost inconsequential compared to those raised by the Central Arizona Project or the Los Angeles Aqueduct, but bringing water to thirsty residents is not at all inconsequential and may become a life-or-death matter in a couple of decades — or sooner, if some of the predictions about global warming come to pass.

The Perils of Groundwater Pumping

Groundwater pumping is just starting to become a part of the national debate. Hydrologists and geophysicists have known for years of the inherent problems with taking water from underground sources. Many water utilities take drinking water from wells. Some wells are deep; others are shallow. Both come with a set of health and environmental problems.

Water taken from far underground contains various toxic compounds: selenium and other salts, arsenic, fluoride, and radioactive elements (U235 and others) referred to as radio-nuclides. These compounds are contained in rocks, and the higher temperatures deeper in the earth cause them to become soluble. Bringing the water containing these compounds and elements to the surface creates a number of problems for human health; many of the compounds are carcinogenic, and radionuclides particularly so. Deep-well pumping also depletes the fossil water (water that was deposited in earlier eons) in aquifers, which, as explained in chapter 2, is potentially fatal. For the most part, deep aquifers are not replenished, and any continual withdrawal eventually depletes an aquifer. The problems created by deep-well pumping, while incremental, are long lasting and often unsolvable.

As problematic as deep-well pumping is to aquifers, it is shallow-well groundwater pumping that causes the most dramatic and immediate problems.[36] The foremost problem of this practice is subsidence — that is, the sinking of the soil that occurs when the water level beneath it drops. When the groundwater is removed or the water table is lowered, the ground above that area subsides like a cork floating on water. The problem is compounded when groundwater pumping occurs under or adjacent to heavily populated areas, as it usually does. That is exactly what has happened in both the San Joaquin Valley in California, and the Tampa Bay area in Florida. Subsidence in the San Joaquin Valley has been the most dramatic: The land surface dropped between 20 and 35 feet in about fifty years, and residences and other buildings have sustained heavy damage.[37] Near Picacho, Arizona, as the land subsided from shallow-well groundwater pumping, huge cracks appeared on the land — one of these is not a mere crack, but a fissure that in 2004 measured more than 10 miles long and at least 100 feet deep. This crevice varies in width from 1 to 30 feet, and the width increases as the surface keeps eroding.[38]

New Orleans has subsided by at least 10 feet in its outlying areas (where the groundwater pumping of water was exacerbated by oil and gas extraction).[39] It is estimated that New Orleans itself is subsiding by at least 1 inch per year;[40] that isn't much on an annual basis, but it is quite a bit over a decade or century. Structural damage has already occurred, and the U.S. Army Corps of Engineers now acknowledges that the design of any flood-control measures — levee reconstruction, for example — will need to take this subsidence into consideration.[41] While subsidence in New Orleans is in part a natural occurrence, it has been exacerbated by human tinkering with the natural flow of other bodies of water that affect the area. Historically, as the lands around New Orleans subsided, sediment carried in by the Mississippi River negated or neutralized the effect, and the elevation remained relatively constant. Now, however, most of the sediment of the Mississippi River (greatly reduced by dams on the Missouri) is carried out to sea and no longer replenishes the New Orleans area.

The second problem with shallow-well groundwater pumping is the lowering of the water table, which has the effect of draining streams and lakes. This problem is just as dramatic as subsidence, though not as immediate and thus difficult to prove; lawsuits have been brought with that claim, some successful, some not. Subsidence has a direct and legally traceable cause, which isn't the case with the lowering of the water table. If the water table is above the elevation of the stream or lake, water will flow laterally toward these, and either augment the flow or stabilize the lake. In most regions of the country, this is the process that occurs. But as groundwater pumping lowers the water table, the flow of water changes direction. Once the water table is below the elevation of the river, water flows from the river toward the aquifer, replenishing the aquifer but emptying the river. The most dramatic example of this may be viewed in western Kansas, on the Cimarron River, which is now dry except during heavy rains, when once it ran perpetually full. As the water table dropped due to depletion of the Ogallala Aquifer, the springs and seeps that contributed to the flow of the Cimarron dried up.

This is identical to what groundwater pumping did to the Santa Cruz River, a pleasant stream that once flowed through Tucson with willow and cottonwood trees and various shrubs lining its banks. Groundwater pumping literally sucked water from this stream and produced horrible environmental consequences. The pumping lowered the level of the water table below the elevation of the river. The flow in the river disappeared, as did water-dependent species. Then the willow and cottonwood trees and the shrubs died as groundwater pumping lowered the water table below the root zone of the vegetation. What is now present is a dry streambed surrounded by the skeletons of dead trees and bushes.

A number of rivers, streams, and lakes have gone completely dry due to excessive groundwater pumping. Others that have run perpetually for generations now undergo long periods in which water does not flow. Robert Glennon, the author of *Water Follies*, writes that "groundwater pumping has dried up or degraded 90 percent of [Arizona's] once perennial desert streams, rivers, and riparian habitats."[42] There has been a good deal of litigation around this issue in the hardest-hit areas of the country, mostly from disgruntled homeowners who purchased a residence on a lake, only to see the lake go dry. While most of these suits have been fairly recent and are still making their way through the courts, some have been settled (with the usual "don't talk about it" clause), and others have been decided in favor of the property owners. The biggest hurdle for attorneys is to show a "hydrological connection" between a dried-up lake and activities that lowered the water table.

The desert Southwest is not the only area ravaged by groundwater pumping. Along eastern and western coastal areas, including Florida, the Central Valley of California, and the Edwards Aquifer in Texas, groundwater pumping has allowed salt-laden seawater to encroach shallow aquifers, rendering the water taken from these areas unfit to drink. This water exceeds the maximum contaminant levels for safe drinking water established by the U.S. Environmental Protection Agency; it tastes terrible and is harmful to human health. One solution is to pump freshwater into these aquifers. But where does that water come from? Additional groundwater pumping. And so the vicious and destructive cycle continues.

'Bergs and Bladders: Towing Ice and Water

A number of far-fetched schemes have been thought up by desperate water system administrators trying to bring freshwater to their communities. While most of these solutions have been proposed to bring relief to the coastal cities of the West, these exemplify the dire nature of water shortages and can thus serve as warning signs for areas all across the nation.

Again, we turn to the struggles of San Diego.[43] That city and the county of the same name are in the forefront of many high-tech solutions to water woes. Of course, San Diego is not alone in its search. Similar tales could be told about Phoenix, Las Vegas, Albuquerque, and other cities of the desert Southwest. Many other cities in the rapidly growing areas of southern California are engaged in bitter feuds over dwindling supplies of water. Sacramento, Bakersfield, San Bernardino, Barstow, Fresno, Modesto, San Francisco — the list goes on and on — all have their tales of water woes, and each is searching for solutions. So when San Diego is used as an example, it is just that: an example. Substitute for the name "San Diego" any other southwestern city near the Pacific Ocean, and the problem is the same: water is in short supply and high demand.

Spurring its search for more water is the San Diego County

Water Authority's recognition that the public, the city officials, and the local industry have deemed growth and development as necessary. In order to meet the requirements of a growing population and to attract industries, ever-increasing supplies of water are needed. Those are difficult to come by in a land of little rain. San Diego County's annual rainfall totals 10 to 14 inches,[44] but most of its drinking water comes from outside the county. Large reservoirs store the water from the mountains on the more precipitous eastern side of the county, but those reservoirs contribute less than 20 percent of the water supply.[45]

In what sounds like the act of desperation it was, as a result of legislation adopted by the California Assembly in 1978 to endorse the notion of towing icebergs to meet drinking water needs,[46] San Diego County investigated the possibility of towing icebergs from the Arctic Ocean to just offshore and tapping the water stored in this ice. Icebergs do contain millions of gallons of freshwater, as they are pure offshoots of glaciers formed by compressed Arctic snow. Of the 3 percent of Earth's water that is fresh, or potable, water, about 70 percent is contained in icebergs, glaciers, and ice sheets of the polar regions.[47] The enormous amounts of water now melting from ice in the polar regions are of the most concern in discussions, reports, and scientific papers on global warming issues.

In researching the feasibility of towing icebergs from the Arctic Ocean, San Diego County Water Authority staffers learned quite a bit. The glaciers of the Arctic move slowly down from their mountainous origins and break off into large chunks — icebergs — upon reaching the ocean. Size is quite variable — from monsters that would dwarf Rhode Island to ones that would fit in a rowboat.

A similar occurrence happens in Antarctica, but the icebergs there are so massive that the larger ones would have to be broken into towable-size pieces. In addition, it is much farther from Antartica to San Diego than from the Arctic to San Diego. While engineers and scientists acknowledge that moving icebergs from Antarctica to warm and dry climes is possible, so far the logistics have proven insurmountable.[48]

Still, while the icebergs in Alaska's Arctic are much more manageable in size, and while it is a much shorter distance from Alaska to Southern California, the costs remain prohibitive. Operating an oceangoing towboat is quite expensive — on the order of $14,000 per day for a tug that has a 10,000-horsepower engine.[49] Given that the tug would be making a round trip that would take at least twenty-eight days, the cost for the towing alone would be a minimum of $392,000. Since icebergs are difficult to steer, it is also likely that at least two large tugs would be needed, meaning that the price would double. This amount does not include the equipment needed to lasso and secure the iceberg for towing.

Another as yet insurmountable problem is simple survival. The Pacific Ocean is known for its turbulent waters. Towing an iceberg — unwieldy, unstable, and not conducive to straight-ahead movement[50] — would add to an already difficult problem. While there are tugs capable of dealing with the rough seas in the Pacific, as yet these have not been called on to tow anything the size of an iceberg for the distances required. It is telling that very few owners of large vessels have responded to requests for proposals to tow icebergs.

The third problem is actually a set of problems that relate to environmental harm.[51] Icebergs are cold and would lower the surrounding marine temperature by several degrees. While this does not pose a problem in the already cold Arctic Ocean, this does present a considerable problem in the much warmer waters of the Pacific off the states of Washington, Oregon, and California. Harm to marine life — fish and plants — from this colder water would be immense and would hurt local fisheries. This would especially be the case when the iceberg was stationary at its destination. In addition to the harm that would result from colder surrounding temperatures, there is considerable concern about damage to the ocean bottom. Since about seven-eighths of an iceberg sits below the surface of the seawater, if the iceberg were towed close to shore, the iceberg would be likely to scrape the bottom and would wipe out any marine life that depended upon the ocean floor for life at any or all stages of its cycle.[52] Finally, there is the problem of getting the iceberg's freshwater into the pipes of a water utility. Various solutions have been suggested, but most involve breaking the iceberg into manageable pieces, and these would in turn harm the surrounding sea life.

While most of the problems with moving icebergs from the polar zones could be solved (although there are obviously nagging technical and environmental problems), ultimately the costs are prohibitive. If freshwater from icebergs is to be utilized, the cost of water would soar. Again, only those with considerable wealth would be able to afford a large supply of freshwater. People on fixed incomes or below the poverty line would be able to afford water only for drinking.

When the San Diego County Water Authority realized that towing icebergs wasn't economically possible, the county looked seriously at towing water in gigantic bladders — 800 feet long, 200 feet wide and 25 feet deep — carrying about 46.5 acre-feet of water each, for a total of 15 million gallons. The idea was that the water would come to San Diego this way rather than through a pipeline, which would be costly.

The first proposal was to tow water from Mendocino County's Albion and Gualala rivers, but that was rejected by the California Coastal Commission as a result of the vigilance of a few citizens who led an outcry that resonated with the commission. Were it not for those citizens, chances are that the somewhat shaky proposition would have been approved. There still would have been a remaining problem with the San Diego County Water Authority and its ability or willingness to pay the high rates for such water, but things never got that far.

The current proposal is to bring water from Humboldt County, California — which has plenty of water to spare in its Mad River. Right now, San Diego pays around $400 per acre-foot and Humboldt County's water costs are less than half that (a bit less than $200 per acre-foot), but quick calculations revealed that water delivered from Humboldt County would cost about $5,000 per acre-foot just for the towboat costs. Ric Davidge, head of Alaska Water, the company proposing to deliver water from Humboldt County to San Diego,[53] states that this system has been successful in hauling water from Turkey to Cyprus. What the company doesn't admit is that there is a huge difference between towing a water bladder on the peaceful Mediterranean Sea for a distance of less than 100 miles and towing the same bladder on the turbulent Pacific between Humboldt and San Diego — a distance of about 650 miles.

To date, there are no water bladder–towing systems operating in this country, although a few such systems tow water, with the assistance of considerable amounts of international aid money, to isolated islands such as Cyprus.[54] At some point, it could well be that San Diego and other southwestern cities become so desperate for water that they will pay any amount. At that point, water will become a luxury for the very rich.

It should be noted that all the desperate solutions that involve transporting water from faraway sources are designed only for drinking water. While water for irrigation does not have to meet the high standards of drinking water, so far very little attention has been given to the needs of irrigated agriculture. It could be argued that water now used for drinking will instead be diverted to agriculture, but that does not hold true. The proposals detailed above are not meant to replace existing water, but to find new sources to supplement existing drinking water.

At this point, it is highly unlikely that much attention will be devoted to providing water for agricultural uses. It is almost certain that water-dependent crops such as rice will no longer be grown in California or the desert Southwest, as the Central Valley Aquifer is depleted and the coastal cities are demanding more of the water stored in reservoirs in the Sierra. While estimates of the ultimate date of complete desertification vary considerably (from a few years to a century or so), in some formerly fertile areas that time is now, as salt deposits have rendered those areas unfit for growing anything, not even sagebrush or creosote bushes. It is also certain that in Southern California — around the Salton Sea — millions of acres now nourished by irrigation will lie fallow and return to sagebrush and cactus,[55] if these species can reproduce in areas of high soil-salt content.

Water, Water Everywhere

While each of the technologies in this chapter takes a wildly different approach than the others, the one trait they share is their high cost, and — if we end up relying on any of these technologies in earnest, as it appears we will if we don't stop our water-wasting ways immediately — each of us will bear the financial costs in various ways.

In western urban areas, there is little doubt that the cost of water will increase dramatically. Perhaps only the wealthy will be able to afford ample amounts of pure clean water, and poor folks will receive only an amount sufficient to serve their daily needs (estimated by the United Nations to be about 50 liters per day). It is this division that many predict will lead to physical strife — literal water wars. The division will not just be between rich and poor nations, such as the United States and Mexico, but also between rich and poor citizens and between cities and towns in the west. The Los Angeles area contains several havens of extremely wealthy individuals — in Santa Monica, Beverly Hills, the outlying areas of Pasadena, and even Long Beach — but it also includes areas of abject poverty in Downey and East Los Angeles, and in the midst of affluence in Orange County.[56] While movie stars in Beverly Hills bask in hot tubs, mothers in East L.A. will be pondering how many of their children can be bathed in the same water. This same scenario will be played out in the San Francisco Bay Area, and in San Diego, Phoenix, and Las Vegas. At some point, it could well be that those without ample supplies of water will become so resentful that physical attacks will be launched upon those with plenty.

In addition to the water shortages for personal use, individual citizens will have to cope with the skyrocketing costs of food, since none of these technological solutions will address the water needs of irrigated agriculture.[57] When water costs become so high that only the wealthy can afford ample water for basic human needs, farmers and ranchers will not be able to make enough profit off the shrinking customer base, and many will go out of business or raise crops that aren't water dependent (or not nearly as profitable as the current ones). Water shortages for agriculture are no trivial matter: the same areas that are so short of water are also the major suppliers of the fruits and vegetables we eat in this country. While the agricultural irrigation component of this problem is not yet an immediate crisis, it will become one as the thirsty residents of western cities use up the water that is typically diverted for crops.

As we consider each of the high-tech solutions discussed

in this chapter, weighing the pros and cons of each, it should be noted that at least two of these technologies — EDR and towing water (whether icebergs or bladders) — would almost inevitably place drinking-water supplies into the hands of for-profit companies. It is foolhardy to rely upon those driven by profit to deliver water on a reliable basis. If costs become too high, the water will not be delivered unless a carefully worded contract calls for extreme penalties for such failures. In these precarious times, it is especially imperative that drinking-water supplies are controlled by the public rather than a company driven by the profit motive.

[WHAT YOU CAN DO]

The episode involving the proposal to tow huge water bladders from Mendocino to San Diego is instructive. Bureaucratic entities — in this instance, the California Coastal Commission — tend to pay attention to the concerns of citizens; if those concerns are not aired, the entity listens primarily to the industrial leaders and, lacking other information, will act upon the advice of such leaders. The key to environmental- and human-friendly decisions (as opposed to profit-driven decisions) is citizen involvement, and that involvement must be appropriate to the situation. In some cases, it may be necessary to contact U.S. representatives or senators; in other situations, it may be crucial to gain the ear of local elected officials. In matters as large as the water bladder proposal, it took two groups of citizens — one in San Diego and one in Mendocino — to defeat the proposal to haul water down the coast.

Persons concerned about water supply and consumption need to watch for proposals that increase water rates. If the water-bladder proposal had not been rejected by the California Coastal Commission, there would have been a call to raise rates. The increase in rates caused by bringing water 650 miles to San Diego would have been dramatic. Not only did folks in Mendocino object to "their" water being transported, but folks in San Diego also objected to the likely rate increases. Unless there is an organized outcry, the water authority will assume that the rate is acceptable to the citizenry and probably go through with a contract. But if there is an outcry, the water authority may reject the proposal and find other, less costly sources of water. Citizen involvement is the primary reason that the San Diego County Water Authority is investigating desalination and has made a commitment that water rates will not dramatically increase.

It is not necessary to closely follow on a daily, weekly, or even monthly basis the proceedings of a local water authority. Governmental agencies are required to post legal notices in a newspaper of general circulation. Keeping informed may mean subscribing to the local newspaper, or demanding that local politicians and water providers publish this kind of information on a public utilities website. If there is a proposal for some scheme to bring in new water, and that proposal calls for a dramatic increase in water rates, it is time to call on others with like concerns. While there are national groups that deal with water issues, they should be viewed primarily as sources of information, not of local activism. In the end, the action of local citizens has the most impact. The California Coastal Commission could safely ignore organizations based in Washington, but when citizens in the affected areas got involved, it made all the difference. You, too, can make such a difference.

AFTERWORD

Immediate Collective Action
Is Our Only Hope

We end, then, where we started. The United States, the most powerful and influential country on the planet, is running out of water. While we spend millions in subsidies, research, and development on ethanol, hydrogen, and other alternative fuels (all the while subsidizing the oil and gas industries to the tune of about \$5 billion[1]), our nation is largely neglecting to address the approaching scarcity of water.

This book has detailed the dire straits of citizens from the Atlantic to the Pacific — along with some of the more promising and reasonable proposals to alleviate the impact of our water shortages. From the depletion of aquifers from groundwater pumping, to interstate squabbles over river water rights, to intrastate feuds over the conflicting needs of urban dwellers and big agriculture, water, or rather a lack of it, is demanding our collective attention. Ultimately, it may not be a shortage of oil that becomes a matter of grave concern, but a shortage of water.

Many solutions have been proposed: more reservoirs, more pipelines, more pumping, the conversion of seawater to freshwater, even tugging icebergs from polar regions. All have encountered serious, perhaps insurmountable, problems. There are almost no places left to site dams — every river worth damming has been dammed. Ditto with pipelines. While there are pipelines in place that take water from where it is to where it is needed, few places are untapped — and bordering countries, states, water districts, and municipalities would rather fight decades-long court battles than try to share or conserve what they view as "their" water.

Groundwater pumping has already resulted in lowering and depleting aquifers and is causing millions of dollars in damage from sinkholes caused by subsidence; it is unlikely that aquifer or groundwater sources will be able to supply water in the near future. Towing icebergs from the Arctic or Antarctic is an unworkable pipe dream — costly in terms of delivery and lives. Desalination is somewhat promising, but the potable water thus produced is at this point very costly. In addition, such plants require long periods to obtain permits and require even longer periods to be constructed. It could well be, however, that experimentation, research, and development will eventually result in a relatively inexpensive and almost inexhaustible source of freshwater. The one caveat is that farmers and ranchers will not benefit from this water on an affordable basis — the water produced from desalination is designed only for the essential needs (drinking, bathing, cooking) of urban and suburban residents. This leaves us with the pressing question of how we will continue to produce an adequate food supply for our ever-growing population.

We turn, then, of necessity to conservation. While there should be a sound and comprehensive national policy based on the conservation of all natural resources, with incentives for reduction, that is not in the cards. U.S. Vice President Dick Cheney stated on May 1, 2001, that "conservation may be a sign of personal virtue, but it is not a sufficient basis for a sound, comprehensive energy policy."[2] While the vice president may have been speaking of energy, and President Bush later focused his comments on our country's addiction to oil, it is clear by their stance on those matters that at least for the near future there will be no national leadership on conservation of any natural resources.

There have been some attempts by the U.S. Department of Agriculture to provide incentives for farmers and ranchers who give up their water rights for irrigation,[3] although this has taken place mainly in the western pilot states of New Mexico, Arizona, and west Texas — areas that are quickly depleting or overappropriating their water supplies. So far, there have been few takers, particularly in the areas most at issue. Farmers and ranchers seem to be gambling that they'll make more on crop and animal production by retaining their water rights than they will selling these to the government. A good idea — but one that hasn't achieved much in the way of lessening demand for water.

Lacking federal leadership, the "national program" of conservation must be, de facto, a citizens' program. It falls upon everyone to use water sparingly. No more thirty-minute showers, no more lawn watering, no more filling the bathtub to the top. While perhaps slightly inconvenient, none of these changes are all that burdensome, especially considering the stringent measures in our future if we don't conserve now. For now, water conservation does not mean elimination, simply reasonable reduction. A change in attitude will certainly be needed. Rather than being used as a recreational activity, a hot shower must be used only for cleansing — which doesn't take nearly as long. Rather than a lawn of lush green grass, the front yard could be green gravel or plants that are not water dependent (or, at least, watered with "gray water" that has already been used for laundry and the like). In particular, it makes little sense for folks in the desert cities of Phoenix, Tucson, Las Vegas, and Albuquerque to grow grass for close-clipped mowing — and indeed the water utilities of those towns are encouraging conversion around these water-wasting practices.[4]

Farmers and ranchers in areas where waters come from deep aquifers or shallow groundwaters will eventually be forced, when the water runs out altogether, to switch to crops that are not reliant on irrigation; of course, it would be better if those changes were made now. It is always easier to make transitions when they are voluntary rather than mandatory. If the wells run dry, no smooth transition is possible, and going from cotton, soybeans, corn, and milo in one year to dryland wheat and oats the next is not an easy change for farmers to make. Irrigated agriculture and dryland farming call for vastly different techniques and equipment. But if those farmers and ranchers insist on pressing on in the same manner, refusing to heed the reality of today's water supply, then one day soon they'll wake up and find that their huge pumps and irrigation systems will be of little use, because there will be no water for them to extract. In the end, it falls on a vigilant citizenry to watch those entities that we have entrusted with our water supplies. The goal of those agencies is to supply ever-increasing amounts of water to promote growth and development, while the goal of citizens is to ensure that there's enough to supply current users. If there is barely enough water now, water agencies will find it increasingly difficult to provide enough to continue the current rate of growth and development. It is by no means a sure thing, for example, that Las Vegas will secure water from White Pine County. Not only do the residents of White Pine County have reason to be concerned about their water being diverted to Las Vegas, but the citizens of Las Vegas have reason to be concerned about what will happen if this water is not piped to their burgeoning metropolis. This proposal is indeed a double-edged sword.

While Phoenix has taken steps to require that developers of new subdivisions provide assurance of a water supply for a hundred years,[5] the individual water utility administrators, the developers, and the buyers of homes in the subdivision will not be around in a hundred years. The question then arises of how this commitment will be enforced; and since everyone involved knows this, what's to stop the developers and the city officials from stepping into deals that don't benefit future citizens? When the water stops flowing, who will be held accountable? And even if someone *is* held accountable and is ordered to pony up some big bucks, the water will be gone by then, and money is no substitute for water.

Likewise, elected officials are no substitute for an alert citizenry. Elected officials are accountable to those who give the most money to their electoral campaigns and will work to ensure that the donors are rewarded with a deep sip. Likewise, the directors of state and federal agencies are beholden to those who put them in these positions, and if politics dictates that the casinos of Las Vegas or the developers of Phoenix receive ample amounts of water, then the Colorado River will be apportioned accordingly.

We live in a democracy. Politicians should make decisions about water appropriations that benefit everyone — not just a select few. Certainly, the media should hold these elected officials accountable and carry stories about their catering to the rich, influential, and powerful. But that ain't gonna happen — especially since the rich, influential, and powerful now own the bulk of the media. So it's up to us, the everyday folks, the common citizens, to make a difference. It's up to you.

Were it not for a group of alert and committed citizens in Lexington, Kentucky, and Stockton, California, the water delivery systems of those towns would have been turned over to private for-profit companies. Were it not for a group of alert and committed citizens in upstate New York, it is likely that our nation's largest city would have been forced to construct a costly water treatment system, after the pristine wilderness and water source it depends on was destroyed so someone could make money.

Now we need to direct our attention to the woes of the Rio Grande and Colorado, the Missouri and the Apalachicola. The water has to be sent where it is most needed, and that must be decided collectively; if local or basinwide decisions stall, the federal government should mediate. If that means a few farmers in California's Imperial Valley don't get water for irrigation, then that is a decision that should be made in Southern California by citizens — not in the backrooms of a congressional office in Washington, D.C. Citizens nationwide also need to insist that Las Vegas and Phoenix take drastic steps in curbing their unsustainable population growth, while ensuring that development (without growth) continues.

The decisions facing citizens will not be easy ones, but these decisions are much too important to be left in the hands of politicians. In order for us to continue having enough drinking water and food, citizens must become involved and take the reins away from those who would continue to ensure that water flows only toward money. We must push hard for the establishment of national conservation programs that truly conserve, allocate water to those most in need, and call for a halt of wasteful and unnecessary projects. Water is too precious, too valuable to be entrusted to for-profit companies and transient politicians. Water is too essential to be wasted. Water is life.

ACKNOWLEDGMENTS

If there are any mistakes in this book, I take full responsibility for them, and in no way should the persons who provided information be held accountable for my interpretation of what they told me.

I am much indebted to Paul and Kerri Elders — leaders of the Concerned Citizens for Clean Water; originally of Clovis, New Mexico, and now living in Cloudcroft, New Mexico — for much information on the large dairies of that state and the depletion and pollution of the southernmost reaches of the Ogallala Aquifer. Likewise to Marilyn and Clarence Yanke of the Texas Panhandle. Many others gave of their time to speak with me or to send me letters and emails regarding the drawdown of the Ogallala.

Speaking at length with Rich Ingebretsen and Dave Wegner and reading their thoughtful words on the webpages of the Glen Canyon Institute, as well as exchanging emails with John Horning of the Forest Guardians, filled some gaps in my knowledge of the Colorado and Rio Grande rivers. In addition, although they probably won't like to be acknowledged in this book, the Friends of Lake Powell were of much assistance.

It is my great privilege to have a friendship with Wendell Berry. His kind words of advice and his books about local food production and the economies of rural communities have been invaluable. In addition, my tour of the Missouri River floodplain farm, conducted by an anonymous farmer (who wants it that way), was also helpful, and his time was much appreciated. Also much appreciated were the thoughts of Ron Kucera (former deputy director of the Missouri Department of Natural Resources) and Bill Lambrecht (Washington bureau chief of the *St. Louis Post-Dispatch*).

Providing assistance with other issues were Al Gore (unbeknownst to him), an anonymous executive of a private water company, several public utility managers, Chad Smith at the American Rivers organization, Mark Reynolds, Ray Donnell, Joe Hargrave (wherever he may be), and the "Wilsons."

Finally, I would be remiss if I failed to mention the unflagging support of Taryn Fagerness at the Sandra Dikjstra Literary Agency and that of Angela Watrous, who edited my fumbling words and helped bring a semblance of organization and sensibility to chaos. If the concepts and opinions in this book appear knowledgeable, it is mostly due to Angela. If, on the other hand, this book appears confused and filled with nonsense, those failings are mine.

NOTES

Foreword

1. J. B. Moyle, trans., *The Institutes of Justinian* 2.1.1, 4th ed. (Oxford: Clarendon Press, 1906).

2. *The Commentaries on the Laws of England of Sir William Blackstone,* 4th ed. (London: J. Murray, 1876), 33–34.

3. "Comment, the Public Trust in Tidal Areas: A Sometime Submerged Traditional Doctrine," *Yale Law Journal* 79:4 (1970): 762, 789.

4. M. Bloch, *French Rural History* (Berkeley: University of California Press, 1966), 183.

5. H. Schultes, *An Essay on Aquatic Rights* (Philadelphia: J. S. Littell, 1839), 10.

6. J. Angell, *A Treatise on the Right of Property in Tide Waters and in the Soil and Shores Thereof* (Boston: H. Gray, 1826), 33–34.

7. Northwest Ordinance, ch. 8, 1 *United States Statutes at Large*, 50, 52 (1789).

Introduction

1. This has been written about recently by Howard Harris in "Food Shortages and Higher Prices Coming?" *Alpha Omega Report*, June 13, 2006, http://aoreport.com/mag/index.php?option=com_content &task=view&id=262 &Itemid=44.

2. North Plains Groundwater Conservation District, http://www.npwd.org/new_page_2.htm.

3. MindBit, "Johnstown Flood," http://johnstown-flood.mindbit.com/.

4. *New Perspectives on the West*, s.v. "William Mulholland," The West Film Project and WETA, 2001, para. 12, http://www.pbs.org/weta/thewest/people/i_r/mulholland.htm.

5. For 1950: U.S. Bureau of the Census, *Census of Population Vol. 1: Number of Inhabitants*, http://www2.census.gov/prod2/decennial/documents/23761117 v1ch03.pdf, p. 2. For 2006: U.S. Bureau of the Census Question & Answer Center, "The 300 Million Milestone," https://ask.census.gov/cgi-bin/askcensus.cfg/php/enduser/std_ adp.php?p_faqid=1117.

6. 1993 Food Industry Environmental Conference, *Survey of Water Use in the California Food Processing Industry*, p. 221, http://www.p2pays.org/ref/13/12908.pdf.

7. See the summer 2004 newsletter issued by the Western Environmental Law Center, http://www.westernlaw.org/news/newsletters/Welc%20NL%20summer%2004.pdf.

8. Every language has its version of this: in Spanish, *el agua es vida*; French, *l'eau, c'est la vie*, and so forth. For "water equals life" in many other languages, see http://www.word2word.com/howto/waterad.html.

Chapter 1

1. U.S. Geological Survey, Colorado Water Science Survey, http://co.water.usgs.gov/Website/projects/viewer.htm.

2. Aldo Leopold, *Sand County Almanac: And Sketches Here and There* (New York: Oxford University Press, 1949).

3. City of Yuma, Arizona, http://www.ci.yuma.az.us/water _quality.htm.

4. Environmental Defense, "The Colorado River Delta," http://www.environ mentaldefense.org/article.cfm?ContentID=2641.

5. U.S. Department of the Interior, "Call for Proposals for the 2006 CALFED Water Use Efficiency Grants Program," http://www.usbr.gov/newsroom/newsrelease/detail.cfm?RecordID=10421.

6. U.S. Geological Survey, http://www/waterdata.usgs.gov/ut/nwis/sw.

7. Friends of Lake Powell, http://www.lakepowell .org/page_two/information/25_reasons/25_reasons.html.

8. Glen Canyon Institute, http://www.glencanyon.org/aboutgci/history.php.

9. U.S. Department of the Interior, Bureau of Reclamation, "The Law of the River," http://www.usbr.gov/lc/region/g1000/lawofrvr.html; click "The Colorado River Compact of 1922" for a PDF file.

10. Antelope Point Holdings, "Antelope Point Marina," http://www.azmarinas.com/AntelopePoint/.

11. U.S. Geological Survey, http://md.usgs.gov/drought/define.html.

12. Glen Canyon Institute, http://www.glencanyon.org/.

13. Friends of Lake Powell, http://www. lakepowell.org.

14. U.S. National Park Service, Glen Canyon National Recreation Area, "Lake Powell Pure Now & Forever," http://www.nps.gov/glca/lpp.htm.www.americanparknetwork.com/parkinfo/content.asp?catid=68&content typeid=44.

15. Information in this paragraph was taken from climatological studies by the University of Arizona (http://www.uapress.arizona.edu/BOOKS/bid1540.htm), University of Colorado (http://www.leeds.colorado.edu/), U.S. Geological Survey (http://www.pubs.usgs.gov/fs/2002/fs119-02/fs119-02.pdf), and Brigham Young University (http://www.geog.byu.edu/faculty/faculty_staff).

16. U.S. Department of the Interior, Bureau of Reclamation, "The Colorado River Compact of 1922," http://www.usbr.gov/lc/region/g1000/pdfiles/crcompct.pdf.

17. U.S. Library of Congress, Hispanic Reading Room, "The Treaty of Guadalupe Hidalgo," http://www.loc.gov/rr/hispanic/ghtreaty/.

18. Glen Canyon Institute, "Assessing Implications of Operating the Colorado River Resource System with and without Glen Canyon Dam," http://www.glencanyon.org/library/hydrology2005.pdf.

19. U.S. Geological Survey, http://content.lib.utah.edu/cdm4/item_viewer.php?CISOROOT=/wwdl-er&CISOPTR= 229&REC=2.

20. U.S. Library of Congress, Hispanic Reading Room, "The Treaty of Guadalupe Hidalgo," http://www.loc.gov/rr/hispanic/ghtreaty/.

21. *Brownsville Herald*, May 1999, http://www.twdb.state.tx.us/rwpg/2006_RWP/RegionM/PDF%20Final%20Plan/Chapter%208%20Final%20Plan.pdf.

22. Communication from Lower Rio Grande Valley Sierra Club, March 2006.

23. U.S. Department of the Interior, Bureau of Reclamation, "Lower Colorado River Water Delivery Contracts: Questions and Answers," http://www.usbr.gov/lc/region/g4000/contracts/whatcontract.html.

24. Attributed to Huey Long, Louisiana political kingpin.

25. For more information about recycling water, see U.S. Environmental Protection Agency, "Water Recycling and Reuse: The Environmental Benefits," http://www.epa.gov/Region9/water/recycling/index.html.

26. Much of this information on water conservation was taken from Texas A&M University System and New Mexico State University, *Urban Water Conservation along the Rio Grande: An Inventory of Water Conservation Programs*, http://texaswater.tamu.edu/Resources/water_conservation_along_the_rio_grande.pdf.

Chapter 2

1. Most of the information on the Poppers was derived from Anne Matthews, *Where the Buffalo Roam: Restoring America's Great Plains*, 2nd ed. (Chicago: University of Chicago Press, 2002).

2. Dave Raney, " 'Buffalo Commons' Idea Gets Second Look," *Lawrence Journal-World,* February 9, 2004, http://www2.ljworld.com/news/2004/feb/09/buffalo_commons_idea/. Hayden's remark was reported widely in an Associated Press story in 1987.

3. "Edward Jones" is a pseudonym for a rancher who does not wish to have his true identity revealed. All information on "Rancher Jones" is based on personal communications.

4. Kansas Geological Survey, *An Atlas of the Kansas High Plains Aquifer*, 2000, http://www.kgs.ku.edu/HighPlains/atlas/.

5. Concerned Citizens for Clean Water, "State Engineer's Report 99-2," http://www.saveourwatersupply.org/ogallala/report99-2 .html.

6. U.S. Geological Survey, "Sustainability of Ground-Water Resource in the Upper Arkansas River Basin between Buena Vista and Salida, Colorado, 2000–2003," http://pubs.usgs.gov/fs/2005/3143/.

7. Conversation and correspondence with Larry Wallin, the city manager of Logan, New Mexico, March 2004.

8. According to my interviews with the Elders, March 2004.

9. Jack Lyne, "Big Cheese: New Mexico's Incentives Help Land Glanbia's $192M Plant," *Site Selection,* September, 2003, http://www.siteselection.com/ssinsider/incentive/ti0309.htm.

10. Concerned Citizens for Clean Water, "A Pretty Cheesy Deal," March 8, 2004, http://www.saveourwatersupply.org/cheesy/cheesy_deal.html.

11. City of Dumas, Minutes of City Council Meeting, January 21, 2002.

12. U.S. Bureau of the Census, http://www.census.gov/population/estimates/state/st-99-3.txt.

13. American Friends Service Committee, "Glossary of International Trade Terms," http://www.afsc.org/trade-matters/learn-about/glossary.htm.

14. Raney, "'Buffalo Commons.'"

15. Pete Letheby, "Corn Ethanol Isn't All It's Cracked Up to Be," *Salt Lake Tribune,* May 19, 2006. Reprinted by the Environmental Work Group, http://www.ewg.org/news/story.php?id=5323.

Chapter 3

1. U.S. Department of Agriculture, http://www.usda.gov/factbook/chapter 3.htm.

2. Jeffrey Rothfeder, *Every Drop for Sale: Our Desperate Battle over Water in a World About to Run Out* (New York: Putnam, 2001).

3. Report of the KC District of the US Army Corps of Engineers: "Missouri River Bank Stabilization and Navigation — Fish and Wildlife Mitigation Program," http://www.nwk.usace.army.mil/projects/mitigation/projnews/Corning/CorningDraftMainReport062906.pdf4.

4. "Low Water Levels Spur Corps to Cancel Pulse," *Columbia Tribune,* http://archive.columbiatribune.com/2006/mar/20060302news020.asp.

5. Information derived from various reports of the Missouri State Emergency Management Agency (SEMA after the flood of 1995), http://www.mo.water.usgs.gov/current_studies/SEMA/.

6. U.S Geological Survey, "Missouri State Emergency Management Agency," http://mo.water.usgs.gov/current_studies/SEMA/.

7. Midwest Climate Water, http://mrcc.sws.uiuc.edu/climate_midwest/mwclimate_data_sum maries.htm.

8. The 100th meridian was described well by Wallace Stegner in his book on John Wesley Powell (*Beyond the Hundredth Meridian*). The 100th meridian is a north-south line of longitude that traverses the middle of the Dakotas, Nebraska, Kansas, and Oklahoma, and divides western from eastern Texas. West of the 100th meridian is a land where rainfall seldom exceeds 20 inches per year, while lands east of the 100th meridian receive more than 20 inches per year. Anything below 20 inches per year will not support agricultural crops.

9. Rothfeder, *Every Drop for Sale*; and Mark Reisner, *Cadillac Desert: The American West and Its Disappearing Water* (New York: Viking Penguin, 1986).

10. U.S. Geological Survey, http://pubs.usgs.gov/sir/.

11. All information on farm subsidies is from the Environmental Working Group, which placed the entire farm subsidy database of the USDA on its site, http://www.ewg.org:16080/farm/index.php?key=nosign.

12. Ibid.

13. Mary Hunter Austin, *The Land of Little Rain* (New York: Houghton Mifflin, 1903).

14. Environmental Working Group, Farm Subsidy Database, http://www.ewg.org:16080/farm/index.php?key=nosign.

15. Ibid.

16. Ibid.

17. Wendell Berry, *What Are People For?* (Berkeley, CA: North Point Press, 1990).

18. A simple illustration can be found at Groundwater Stewardship in Oregon, "Cone of Depression," http://groundwater.orst.edu/under/images/depressionb.html.

19. U.S. Department of Health and Human Services, Office on Smoking and Health, "Tobacco Use in the United States," http://www.cdc.gov/tobacco/overview/tobus_us.htm.

20. Alternative Farming Systems Information Center, http://www.nal.usda.gov/afsic/csa/.

21. Carl Safina, *Song of the Blue Ocean* (New York: Henry Holt 1999).

Chapter 4

1. "Ray Donnell" is a pseudonym for a Bakersfield resident who accompanied me on a tour of the Central Valley.

2. Friends of the River, http://www.friendsoftheriver.org/CaliforniaRivers/Rivers/Kings.html.

3. Both tree species are notorious for taking up immense quantities of water. Tamarisk, in particular, has become the scourge of desert waterways. The Bureau of Land Management has devoted hours and hours to eradication of this invasive species on tributaries of the Colorado River, where it has displaced indigenous species and led to the drying up of miles of previously flowing waterway. The only method for surefire eradication is to chop down mature trees and treat the stumps with a chemical that kills the roots.

4. John Robbins, "Why I Am Joining PETA in Suing the California Milk Board over Their 'Happy Cows Come from California' Ad Campaign," http://www.foodrevolution.org/lawsuit_milkboard.htm.

5. U.S. Environmental Protection Agency, "2001 Progress Report: Agricultural Production Results in the Loss of Unutilized Nutrients Such as Nitrogen (N) and Phosphorus (P) to Ground and Surface Waters," http://es.epa.gov/ncer/fellow/progress/98/dunlap01.html.

6. Reisner, *Cadillac Desert*.

7. Center on Race, Poverty and the Environment, Rural Poverty Water Project, http://www.crpe-ej.org/campaigns/safewater/index.html.

8. SacDelta, "History of the California Delta," http://www.sacdelta.com/hist.html.

9. Bay Area Alliance, http://www.bayareaalliance.org.

10. California Department of Economic Development, "January 2006 Cities/Counties Ranked by Size, Numeric, and Percent Change," May 2006, http://www.dof.ca.gov/HTML/DEMOGRAP/Reports Papers/Estimates/Rankings/CityCounties1-06/Ranker Text.asp.

11. Resources for this section included the Bay Area Water Supply and Conservation Agency (http://www.bawsca.org/) and an organization called Restore Hetch Hetchy (http://www.hetchhetchy.org/).

12. Ronald Reagan's Interior Secretary Ed Meese asserted his support for draining Hetch-Hetchy: See R4694, October 13, 1987, "Hetch Hetchy Dam," *Jennings/Caras* (31:33 ABC) and R4694, October 13, 1987, "Hetch Hetchy Dam in San Francisco," *Rather/Blackstone* (44:50 CBS), http://www.reagan.utexas.edu/archives/audiovisual/whca8789.html.

13. "Mark Reynolds" is a pseudonym.

14. Ardath Dietrich, *Seen from a Saddle,* Mt. Whitney Packers and Owen Valley History Society, http://www.owensvalleyhistory.com/stories1/seen_from_saddle.pdf.

15. Reisner, op. cit.

16. Information on the Colorado River at Yuma was derived from conversations with residents of that hot town and from information on Yuma's website, http://www.ci.yuma.az.us.

17. Joe Gelt, "Sharing Colorado River Water: History, Public Policy and the Colorado River Compact," *Arroyo* 10, no. 1 (August 1997), http://www.ag.arizona.edu/AZWATER/arroyo/101comm.html.

18. U.S. Bureau of the Census: 2000, http://quickfacts.census.gov/qfd/.

19. Central Arizona Project, http://www.cap-az.com/.

20. Phillip Gomez, "Schumacher Sees 'Old' Vegas in Pahrump," *Pahrump Valley Times*, March 8, 2006, http://www.pahrumpvalleytimes.com/2006/03/08/news/schumacher.html.

21. U.S. Department of Interior, "Colorado River Compact, 1922," http://www.usbr.gov/lc/region/g1000/pdfiles/crcompct.pdf.

22. This was reported in many articles from 2004 to the present in various Nevada newspapers, especially the *Las Vegas Sun* and *Las Vegas Review-*

Journal. See, for example, Henry Brean, "Spring Valley: Water Rights, Riches," *Las Vegas Review-Journal,* August 14, 2006, http://www.review journal.com/lvrj_home/2006/Aug-14-Mon2006/news/9003058.html.

23. During May 28–31, 1997, a Colorado River Compact Symposium was conducted at Bishops Lodge in Santa Fe, where compact delegates had met in 1922, to celebrate the seventy-fifth anniversary of the signing of the compact. The symposium topic was "Using History to Understand Current Water Problems." Pat Mulroy made this statement at that conference, according to Gelt, "Sharing Colorado River Water."

24. Clay L. Pierce, "Habitat Use and Population Dynamics of Benthic Fishes along the Missouri River," http://www.cfwru.iastate.edu/projects/com pleted/MoRiv.pdf#search=%22Missouri%20River%204%20Segments%22.

25. Personal conversation with an Iowa farmer in the summer of 2005.

26. Stephen Ambrose, *Undaunted Courage: Meriwether Lewis, Thomas Jefferson, and the Opening of the American West* (New York: Touchstone, 1996).

27. Greg Miller, "Senator Stumps against Spring Rise," *Columbia Daily Tribune,* September 3, 2005, http://www.columbiatribune.com/2005/Sep/2005 0903News001.asp.

28. U.S. Army Corps of Engineers (Northwestern Division), *Prepared Statement for the Public Field Hearing before the United States House Subcommittee on General Farm Commodities and Risk Management,* February 28, 2006, http://www.nwd-mr.usace.army.mil/rcc/reports/pdfs/AgSub committeeTestimony.pdf.

29. "Corps Decides to Retain Plan for Spring Rise," *Columbia Daily Tribune,* February 1, 2006, http://archive.columbiatribune.com/2006/feb/2006 0201news019.asp.

30. Ibid.

31. Bill Lambrecht, *Big Muddy Blues* (New York: St. Martin's Press, 2005).

32. Environmental Defense Fund, "Missouri River Talking Points," http:// www.environmentaldefense.org/documents/2071_MissouriRiverFact Sheet.pdf#search=%22Barge%20traffic%20Missouri% 20River%22.

33. Personal conversation with retired tow operator, March 2003.

34. *St. Louis Post-Dispatch,* January 14, 2005, http://www.stltoday.com/stltoday/ business/stories.nsf/story/EF66F7FB43.

35. American Rivers, "Follow the Money," http://www.americanrivers .org/.

36. There have been many articles about this issue in the *Atlanta Journal-Constitution* and the *Jacksonville* (Florida) *Daily News.* See, for example, Stacy Shelton, "Drought Heats Up State War for Water," *Atlanta Journal-Constitution,* July 23, 2006, http://www.ajc.com/metro/content/metro/ stories/0723meshriver.html.

37. Charles Seabrook, *ITT Industries Guidebook to Global Water Issues: Atlanta and Southeast,* http://www.itt.com/waterbook/atlanta.asp.

38. Unless otherwise noted, the information in this section was taken from many articles published in 2004 and 2005 in the *New York Times*, the *Poughkeepsie Journal*, and the *Phoenician Times*.

39. Belleayre Resort, http://www.belleayreresort.com/.

40. "Resort Compromise," Brian Hollander, *Phoenicia Times,* October 27, 2005. http://www.phoeniciatimes.com/archivesPT/pt10.27.05/phoenicia.html

41. Brian Hollander, "Resort Compromise," *Phoenicia Times*, October 27, 2005, http://www.phoeniciatimes.com/archivesPT/pt10.27.05/followup .html#ResortCompromise.

42. "Lining Up His Allies," *Phoenicia Times*, September 29, 2005, http://www .phoeniciatimes.com/archivesPT/pt9.29.05/phoenicia.html#LiningUp HisAllies.

43. John Nichols, *The Milagro Beanfield War* (New York: Henry Holt, 1974).

Chapter 5

1. For a report on the demonstration, see Mark Stevenson, "17 Detained at Mexico Water Forum Protest," Common Dreams News Center, March 17, 2006, http://www.commondreams.org/headlines 06/0317-06.htm.

2. Geoffrey F. Segal, "Navigating the Politics of Water Privatization," Reason Public Policy Institute, http://www.rppi.org/apr2003/navigatingthepolitics .html.

3. U.S. Geological Survey, "The Water in You," http://ga.water.usgs.gov/edu/ propertyyou.html.

4. U.S. Geological Survey, "Water Use in the United States," http://pubs .usgs.gov/circ/2004/circ1268/.

5. The information on Atlanta is based on many articles in the *Atlanta Journal-Constitution* from 2000 to 2003, interviews with Atlanta residents, and an extensive story aired by the Canadian Broadcasting Company, http://www.cbc.ca/news/features/water/atlanta.html.

6. Jerry Manders, *In the Absence of the Sacred* (San Francisco: Sierra Club, 1992).

7. Public Citizen, http://www.citizen.org/cmep/water.

8. Democracy Now, "World Water Day 2005: Water Privatization in Stockton and Detroit," http://www.democracynow.org/article.pl?sid=05/03/22/ 1530217 and many articles in the *Stockton Record* from 2003 through 2005.

9. Articles in the *Stockton Record* (http://www.recordnet.com) and the San Francisco *Chronicle* (http://www.sfgate.com). For these, and other, articles, see http://www.cccos.org/html/AP.html.

10. Public Citizen, "Water Privatization Backgrounder," http://www.citizen .org/cmep/Water/activist/articles.cfm?ID=9589

11. Brendan O'Shaughnessy, Richard D. Walton, and Tammy Webber, "Water

Company Faces Questions," *Indianapolis Star*, October 7, 2005, http://www.indystar.com/apps/pbcs.dll/article?AID=/20051007/NEWS01/510070557&SearchID=7322264666570.

12. From a brochure included with water bills from Veolia, http://www.veolia waterna.com/about/media/articles.and.white.papers/road.less.traveled.htm.

13. Jack Miller, "More Bad News for Veolia," *NUVO.net*, July 27, 2005, http://www.nuvo.net/archive/2005/07/27/more_bad_news_for_veolia.html.

14. In order for this conversation to occur, I had to promise the official complete anonymity. As you will see, this person's views contain considerable criticism of a competing company, as well as some "insider" views of the for-profit water industry.

15. Shiva has written a number of articles and a book in opposition to water privatization. For an interview with her, see Paolo Scopacasa, "Vandana Shiva: In Her Own Words," *EcoWorld*, March 6, 2004, http://www.eco world.com/Home/Articles2.cfm?TID =346.

16. This number varies considerably. Water companies use much higher numbers than consumer advocates do.

17. Maude Barlow and Tony Clarke, "Water Privatization: The World Bank's Latest Market Fantasy," Global Policy Forum, http://www.globalpolicy .org/socecon/bwi-wto/wbank/2004/01waterpriv.htm. The authors assert that privatization in both Europe and the developing world has resulted in "huge profits, higher prices for water, cut-offs to customers who cannot pay, . . . reduced water quality, bribery, and corruption."

18. Much of the information about water privatization in Lexington was derived from the article "Thirsty in Lexington," on the Sierra Club "Planet Newsletter" page (http://www.sierraclub.org/planet/200503/clubbeat.asp) and from a citizens' group in Lexington opposed to the proposed privatization (see various 2003–2005 articles in the Lexington *Herald-Review*, http://www.kentucky.com, or http://www.serconline.org/waterPrivatization/press.html).

Chapter 6

1. These are pseudonyms. The "Wilsons" value their privacy and live in a remote valley off the grid due to that desire for privacy. They requested that their real names not be used, as well as any other information that might reveal who and where they are.

2. As related by the Wilsons and as confirmed by a visit to their land.

3. *IPCC Third Assessment Report – Climate Change 2001: The Scientific Basis,* http://www.ipcc.ch/pub/pub.htm.

4. National Center for Atmospheric Research, "Drought's Growing Reach: NCAR Study Points to Global Warming as Key Factor," January 10, 2005, http://www.ucar.edu/news/releases/2005/drought_research.shtml.

5. *IPCC Third Assessment Report – Climate Change 2001: The Scientific Basis,* http://www.ipcc.ch/pub/pub.htm.

6. Ibid.

7. For a discussion of how this aspect of human nature affects planning for the future of humankind, see Michael O'Callaghan, *Global Strategy: Promoting the Concept of Sustainability as a Global Goal*, Global Vision's NGO Position Paper for the Second Session of the United Nations Commission on Sustainable Development, May 16–28, 1994, http://www .global-vision.org/un/strategy/index.html.

8. The fish, game, and forestry agencies of various states assert that our forests are recovering due to their efforts. For example, see Missouri Department of Conservation, http://www. mdc.mo.gov/ nathis/lifeweb/forests.htm.

9. Young People's Trust for the Environment, "Global Warming Factsheet," http://news.bbc.co.uk/2/hi/americas/3499500.stm.

10. Natural Resources Defense Council, "What Is Clearcutting?" http://www .nrdc.org/land/forests/fcut.asp.

11. Ibid.

12. *IPCC Third Assessment Report – Climate Change 2001: The Scientific Basis*, http://www.ipcc.ch/pub/pub.htm.

13. Ibid.

14. Ibid. For more information, written in a layperson's language, see Patrick L. Barry, "A Chilling Possibility," *Science@NASA*, National Aeronautics and Space Administration, Marshall Space Flight Center Science and Technology Directorate, http://www.science.nasa.gov/headlines/y2004/ 05mar_arctic.htm.

15. Hillary Mayell, "Is Warming Causing Alaska Meltdown?" *National Geographic News*, December 18, 2001, http://news.nationalgeographic.com/ news/2001/12/1217_alaskaglaciers.html.

16. National Geographic Society, "Climate Change: Pictures of a Warming World," *National Geographic News,* http://news.nationalgeographic.com/ news/2004/12/photogalleries/global_warming/.

17. Bill Lambrecht, "Genetically Modified Rice Won't Be Planted Near Bootheel Fields," *St. Louis Post-Dispatch,* April 16, 2005, http://www.mindfully .org/GE/2005/Anheuser-Busch-Ventria15apr05.htm. Also reported in a number of southeastern Missouri newspapers.

18. *IPCC Third Assessment Report – Climate Change 2001: The Scientific Basis*, http://www.ipcc.ch/pub/pub.htm.

19. Tim Appenzeller and Dennis R. Dimick, "Global Warming: Signs from Earth," *National Geographic News*, September 2004. An excerpt can be found at http://magma.nationalgeographic.com/ngm/0409/feature1/index.html.

20. This can be confirmed by entering "as far as is known" or "further study" along with "climate change" in any search engine.

21. Various reports of the National Center for Atmospheric Research make this clear. For example, see *NCAR as an Integrator, Innovator, and Community Builder: A Strategy-Implementation Plan for the National Center for Atmospheric Research,* January 2006, http://www.ncar.ucar.edu/stratplan06.pdf.

22. Paul Ehrlich and Anne Ehrlich, "Fables about the Atmosphere and Climate," in *Betrayal of Science and Reason*, chap. 9 (Washington, DC: Island Press, 1996).

23. National Climatic Data Center, http://www.ncdc.noaa.gov.

24. Ibid.

25. The Weather Channel, "Monthly Averages for Phoenix, AZ," http://www .weather.com/weather/wxclimatology/monthly/graph/USAZ0166?from= dayDetails_bottomnav_undeclared.

26. City Rating, http://www.cityrating.com/cityhumidity.asp?City=Phoenix.

27. Canadian Institute for Climate Studies, Canadian Climate Impacts Scenarios Group, "Scenario Access," http://www.cics.uvic.ca/scenarios/data/ select.cgi.

28. EPA Regional Conference, "Global Climate Change: What Does it Mean for the Midwest and the Great Lakes?" September 1997, http://yosemite .epa.gov/oar/globalwarming.nsf/UniqueKeyLookup/SHSU5BPKL7/$Fil/ chicago.pdf#search=%22Cooler%20Midwest%20Climate%20change%22.

29. U.S. Geological Survey, *Water Quality in the South Platte River Basin: Colorado, Nebraska, and Wyoming, 1992–95,* pubs.usgs.gov/circ/circ1167/circ 1167.pdf.

30. "Impacts of Climate Change in the United States: Texas and the Southern Great Plains," *Global Warming: Early Warning Signs*, http://www.climate hotmap.org/impacts/texas.html. This website is produced by Environmental Defense, Natural Resources Defense Council, Sierra Club, Union of Concerned Scientists, U.S. Public Interest Research Group, World Resources Institute, and World Wildlife Fund.

31. Natural Resources Defense Council, "Global Warming Threatens Florida," October 23, 2002, http://www.nrdc.org/globalwarming/nflorida.asp.

32. Based on predicted sea level rise as reported in many publications. See, for example, David Biello, "Climate Model Predicts Greater Melting, Submerged Cities," *Scientific American,* March 24, 2006, http://www.sciam .com/article.cfm?articleID=0007FA05-10BC-1423-90BC83414B7F0000.

33. David Perlman, "Global Warming to Affect Water Supply," *San Francisco Chronicle,* June 15, 2001, http://www.sfgate.com/cgibin/article.cgi?file=/ chronicle/archive/2001/06/15/MN167979.DTL.

34. Union of Concerned Scientists, "Confronting Climate Change in California," http://www.ucsusa.org/global_warming/science/confronting-climate- change-in-california.html.

35. Perlman, "Global Warming."

36. As reported by federal agencies concerned about the impacts of global warming. See, for example, U.S. Environmental Protection Agency, "Water Resources," *Global Warming: Impacts,* http://yose mite.epa.gov/oar/global warming.nsf/content/ImpactsWaterResources.html.

37. Brian Handwerk, "Arctic Melting Fast; May Swamp U.S. Coasts by 2099," *National Geographic News,* November 9, 2004, http://news.national geographic.com/news/2004/11/1109_041109_polar_ice.html.

38. According to Al Gore in the movie *An Inconvenient Truth.*

39. Rob L. Evans, "Rising Sea Levels and Moving Shorelines," *Oceanus,* November 16, 2004, http://www.whoi.edu/oceanus/viewArticle.do?id=2484.

40. *The Quotations Page,* http://www.quotationspage.com/quote/26032.html.

41. O'Callaghan, *Global Strategy.*

42. "Poll: Americans See a Climate Problem," *Time,* March 26, 2006, http://www.time.com/time/nation/article/0,8599,1176967,00.html. The poll was conducted by *Time* magazine, ABC News, and Stanford University.

43. Federal Energy Regulatory Commission, http://www.ferc.gov/.

44. Pew Center on Global Climate Change, http://www.pewclimate.org/.

45. Ibid.

46. Environmental Literacy Council, "Automobiles," http://www.enviro literacy.org/article.php/1127.html.

47. Environment News Service, "U.S. Emits Nearly Half World's Automotive Carbon Dioxide," June 28, 2006, http://www.ensnewswire.com/ens/jun2006/2006-06-28-03.asp.

48. Ibid.

49. State of the Union address to the U.S. Congress, January 31, 2006, http://www.whitehouse.gov/stateoftheunion/2006/index.html.

50. U.S. Department of Transportation, National Highway Traffic Safety Administration, "CAFE Overview: Frequently Asked Questions," http://www.nhtsa.dot.gov/cars/rules/cafe/overview.htm.

51. HybridCars, "Sales Numbers," http://www.hybridcars.com/sales-numbers.html.

52. Christine Tierney, "Big SUV Sales Take Dive as Gas Costs Soar," *The Detroit News,* September 2, 2005, http://www.detnews.com/2005/autos insider/0509/02/A01-301633. htm.

53. U.S. Environmental Protection Agency, "EPA's Fuel Economy and Emissions Programs, October 2004, http://www.epa.gov/fueleconomy/420f04053.htm, or see the annual *Consumer Reports* automobile edition.

54. Physicians for Social Responsibility, "Air Pollution and Health: Power Plants," http://www.envirohealthaction.org/pollution/pow er_plants.

55. U.S. Environmental Protection Agency, "Mercury: Health Effects," http://www.epa.gov/mercury/effects.htm.

56. U.S. Department of Energy, Energy Information Administration, "World Carbon Dioxide Emissions from the Consumption of Coal (Million Metric Tons of Carbon Dioxide), 1980–2004," *International Energy Annual 2004,* http://www.eia.doe.gov/iea/carbon.html.

57. Documented by many sources. See, for example, Natural Resources Defense Council, http://www.nrdc.org/OnEarth/05fal/coal1.asp./

58. California is typical in this respect. See California Public Utilities Commission, *Energy Action Plan,* http://www.cpuc.ca.gov/PUBLISHED/REPORT/28715.htm.

59. Central Intelligence Agency, "Rank Order Electricity Consumption," *The World Factbook,* https://www.cia.gov/library/publications/the-world-factbook/rankorder/2042rank.html.

60. Many books and periodicals have outlined a number of steps (usually 50) that can be taken to "save the planet." One good guide is from JustGive: "50 Things You Can Do to Save the Environment," http://www.justgive.org/html/guide/50waysenvironment.html. Another — for youngsters — may be found in the local library or purchased online: Earth Works Group, *50 Simple Things Kids Can Do to Save the Earth* (Kansas City, MO: Andrews and McMeel, 1990).

61. The information in this paragraph was related by "Jim Wilson" and was confirmed by a visit to his residence in June 2004.

62. Karl Stahlkopf, "Taking Wind Mainstream," *IEEE Spectrum Online,* June 2006, http://spectrum.ieee.org/jun06/3544.

63. Carolina Environmental Program, "Policy Options for the Future: Wind Power," http://www.unc.edu/~jrhester/policywind.html.

Chapter 7

1. Much information on the oceans and the water cycle is relayed in Robert Glennon, *Water Follies: Groundwater Pumping and the Fate of America's Fresh Waters* (Washington, DC: Island Press, 2004).

2. Lenntech, "Water Health FAQ," http://www.lenntech.com/Water-Health-FAQ.htm.

3. Ibid.

4. Glennon, *Water Follies.*

5. Susan E. Pantell, "Background," *Seawater Desalination in California,* California Coastal Commission, October 1993, http://www.coastal.ca.gov/desalrpt/dchap1.html.

6. Ibid. For more information on distillation, see The Distillation Group, http://www.distillationgroup.com/distill.htm.

7. Jennifer McNulty, "USCS Desalination Project to Give Cities Tools They Need to Weigh Pros and Cons," *UC Santa Cruz Currents,* July 11, 2005, http://currents.ucsc.edu/05-06/07-11/desalination.asp.

8. Pantell, "Key Desalination Facts," *Seawater Desalination,* http://www.coastal.ca.gov/desalrpt/dkeyfact.html.

9. Pantell, "Potential Environmental Impacts/Coastal Act Issues," *Seawater Desalination,* http://www.coastal.ca.gov/desalrpt/dchap3.html.

10. International Desalination Association, *IDA Desalting Plants Inventory #19*, http://www.idadesal.org/.

11. This system is described in considerable detail by Ionics, http://www.ionics.com/technologies/edr/index.htm.

12. Ibid.

13. San Diego County Water Authority, Agenda for October 27, 2005, item II.2., http://www.sdcwa.org/board/documents/2005_10_27/WP.pdf. Also, Terry Rodgers, "San Onofre Desalination Plant Study Authorized," *San Diego Union-Tribune*, October 28, 2005, http://www.signonsandiego.com/uniontrib/20051028/news_7m28desal.html

14. RBF Consulting, *Regional Seawater Desalination Project at Encina, Sch#2003 091127: Environmental Findings of Fact and Statement of Overriding Considerations;* and *Standard Conditions and Project Design Features and Mitigation Monitoring and Reporting Program for the Regional Seawater Desalination Project at Encina,* a report prepared for the San Diego County Water Authority, June 16, 2006, http://www.sdcwa.org/board/documents/2006_06_22/WP.pdf.

15. Ibid.

16. Rodgers, "San Onofre."

17. San Diego County Water Authority, http://www.sdcwa.org/.

18. San Diego County Water Authority, "Water Management: Water Quality," http://www.sdcwa.org/manage/awmp_07.pdf.

19. San Diego County Water Authority, "Water Management: Conservation Fact Sheet," http://www.sdcwa.org/manage/conservation.phtml.

20. *Water Source* (Newsletter), January 2004, http://www.sdcwa.org/watersource/01_2004.htm.

21. Stegner, *Beyond the Hundredth Meridian.*

22. This was asserted by a number of water rights' attorneys at a convention, Las Vegas, Nevada, April 2005.

23. Theodore A. Endreny, "Sustainability for New York's Drinking Water," *Clearwaters,* Fall 2001, http://www.nywea.org/Clearwaters/pre02fall/313060.html.

24. Reisner, *Cadillac Desert.*

25. U.S. Department of the Interior, Bureau of Reclamation, "Colorado River Basin Project, Central Arizona Project," http://www.usbr.gov/dataweb/html/crbpcap.html.

26. River Lakes, "Lake Mead General Info," http://www.riverlakes.com/lakemead.htm.

27. This has been written about extensively in the Utah press. For a full description, see Richard Ingebretsen, "Lake Powell to St. George Pipeline & Global Warming," *The Canyon Country Zephyr,* April–May 2006, http://www.canyoncountryzephyr.com/april-may2006/pipeline.html.

28. Reisner, *Cadillac Desert*.

29. David Whitford, "Liquid Assets," *Fortune*, January 19, 2006, http://money .cnn.com/magazines/fsb/fsb_archive/2005/12/01/8365369/index.htm. Mesa Water is Mr. Pickens' water company.

30. The text of the Colorado River Compact may be viewed at http://www .usbr.gov/lc/region/g1000/pdffiles/crcompct.pdf.

31. This has generated much controversy and has been covered extensively in the Nevada media. For full and relatively objective accountings, see various stories in the *Las Vegas Sun*, including Cy Ryan, "Water Offer Rejected by White Pine," *Las Vegas Sun*, May 26, 2006, http://www.lasvegas sun.com/sunbin/stories/lv-other/2006/may/26/566625577.html.

32. *Report of the Missouri River Basin Commission*, 1981.

33. U.S. Department of the Interior, Bureau of Reclamation, "PSMBP: Garrison Division," http://www.usbr.gov/dataweb/html/garrison.html.

34. This is a locally controversial matter, covered extensively by the *Desoto Sun*, in Florida, http://www.sun-herald.com.

35. Clifton Park Water Authority, "CPWA Makes Position Known to County," June 9, 2006, http://www.cpwa.org/articlesandinfo.asp?id=14.

36. Most of the information in this section was taken from Glennon, *Water Follies*.

37. U.S. Geological Survey, "Land Subsidence," *Ground Water Atlas of the United States: Segment 1, California Nevada*, http://ca.water.usgs.gov/ groundwater/gwatlas/valley/landsub.html and http://csrc.ucsd.edu/pro jects/sjv.html.

38. Joe Gelt, Jim Henderson, Kenneth Seasholes, et al., "In Search of Adequate Water Supplies," *Water in the Tucson Area: Seeking Sustainability*, Water Resources Research Center, http://cals.arizona.edu/AZWATER/publica tions/sustainability/report_html/chap3_02.html.

39. Paul Noel and Mary-Sue Haliburton, "Unfeasibility of Rebuilding New Orleans," *The Relocalization Network*, September 23, 2005, http://www .earthsky.com/shows/observingearth_interviews.php?id=49221 and http:// www.relocalize.net/node/1126.

40. Virginia R. Burkett, David B. Zilkoski, and David A. Hart, "Sea-Level Rise and Subsidence: Implications for Flooding in New Orleans, Louisiana," U.S. Geological Survey, National Wetlands Research Center, http://www .nwrc.usgs.gov/hurricane/Sea-Level-Rise.pdf.

41. "Rebuilding Levees," *Online NewsHour Special Reports*, Public Broadcasting System, February 16, 2006, http://www.pbs.org/newshour/bb/ science/ jan-june06/levees_2-16.html.

42. Robert Glennon, "The Perils of Groundwater Pumping," *Issues in Science and Technology*, Fall 2002, http://www.issues.org/19.1/glennon.htm.

43. Much of the information on the water woes of San Diego city and county

was taken from the San Diego County Water Authority, http://www.sdcwa.org, and various publications of that authority.

44. National Weather Service, "Average Monthly Weather for San Diego Lindbergh Field," http://www.wrh.noaa.gov/sgx/climate/san-sanmonth.htm.

45. The University of Colorado has several reports on Water Management. See www.colorado.edu:8080, and enter "water management" in the search bar.

46. Charles Howe, "Institutional Innovation in Drought Response," http://www.colorado.edu/conflict/full_text_search/AllCRCDocs/ch2wtpr.htm.

47. U.S. Geological Survey, "The Water Cycle: Water Storage in Ice and Snow," http://ga.water.usgs.gov/edu/watercycleice.html.

48. International Polar Foundation, "Can Icebergs Be Towed?" http://www.antarctica.org/old/UK/Envirn/pag/glaces_UK/oceanes_UK/remorquer_UK.htm.

49. Answers.com, "Towing and Tugboat Services," http://www.answers.com/topic/towing-and-tugboat-services.

50. Provincial Aerospace, Environmental Services Division, "Iceberg Management," http://www.provincialaerospace.com/ESDManagement.htm.

51. Ibid.

52. Stephen E. Bruneau, "Icebergs of Newfoundland and Labrador," http://www.wordplay.com/tourism/icebergs/.

53. Public Citizen, http://www.citizen.org/california/water/gualala/.

54. Peter Gleick, "Safeguarding Our Water," *Scientific American*, February 2001, http://www.mindfully.org/Water/Every-Drop-Count.htm.

55. U.S. Department of Agriculture, Natural Resources Conservation Service, *Water Quality and Agriculture: Status, Conditions, and Trends*, working paper no. 16, July 1997, http://www.nrcs.usda.gov/TECHNICAL/land/pubs/WP16.pdf.

56. Housing Authority of the City of Los Angeles, "Appendix 2: Areas of Minority and Poverty Concentration and Corresponding Rental Ranges," in *2005 Agency Plan*, http://www.hacla.org/public_documents/AdminPlan05/Apx2.htm.

57. Glen Schaible, "Irrigation, Water Conservation, and Farm Size in the Western United States," *Amber Waves*, 2004, http://search.ers.usda.gov/query.html?col=magazine&qt=Schaible%2C+Glenn.

Afterword

1. Taxpayers for Common Sense, "Fossil Fuel Subsidies: A Taxpayer Perspective," http://www.taxpayer.net/TCS/fuelsubfact.htm.

2. Vice President Cheney's remarks on May 1, 2001, were widely reported in the national media from the *New York Times* to the *Los Angeles Times*. For

example, see James Carney and John F. Dickerson, "The Rocky Rollout of Cheney's Energy Plan," *Time*, May 19, 2001, http://www.time.com/time/nation/article/0,8599,127219,00.html.

3. Natural Resources Conservation Service, http://www.nrcs.usda.gov/Programs.

4. For an example of this, see what Tucson is doing: http://www.ci.tucson.az.us/water/conservation.htm.

5. To view the entire document (in Microsoft Word), see "Arizona's Assured Water Supply Rules: Summary, Excerpts from Governor's Water Management Commission Briefing Notebook," August 2000, http://sustainability.asu.edu/docs/water_institute/AWSsummary.doc.

INDEX

Colorado River Aqueduct, 68–69
Colorado River Compact, 5–6,
175n23
Arizona under, 72
Las Vegas under, 70–72,
74–75, 146
"paper water" under, 7
under Treaty of Guadalupe
Hidalgo, 7
"wet water" under, 7
Columbia Plateau basin-fill
aquifer, 23
commons
"Buffalo," 18–20
privatization of, xii
under Roman law, ix–x
Community Supported
Agriculture (CSA), 55
cones of depression, xxi
conservation. *See* water conservation
Constitution, U.S., x
contamination, waterborne,
xvii–xviii
Corporate Average Fuel Economy
(CAFE) standards, 129
Sierra Club and, 130
CSA. (Community Supported
Agriculture), 55

D

dairies
in Central Valley, 59–61
Ogallala Aquifer's relation
to, 26–27
dams
Fort Peck, 78–79
Glen Canyon, xii–xiii, 3–6
Hetch Hetchy Valley, 63–65,
87
Hoover, xii–xiii

Johnstown Flood and, xx
O'Shaughnessy, 63–65
Parker, 68
St. Francis, xx
Davidge, Ric, 156
desalination, 136, 142–43, 162
distillation, 137–38
EDR, 139
EPA funding for, 140–41
inefficiency of, 138–39
reverse osmosis, 137
See also reverse osmosis filtration
distillation, 137–38
drainage ditches, xix
dryland farming, 43
Dust Bowl, 54

E

EDR. *See* electrodialysis reversal
Edwards Aquifer (TX), 23, 152
Ehrlich, Anne, 124
Ehrlich, Paul, 124
Einstein, Albert, 128
Elders, Kerri, 25–26
Elders, Paul, 25–26
electricity consumption
global warming and, 131–32
photovoltaic cell systems
and, 133–34
electrodialysis reversal (EDR),
139
Endangered Species Act, 77
energy sources, alternative
photovoltaic cells, 133–34
wind generation, 133
environmental organizations
Friends of Lake Powell, 3–5
National Wildlife Federation,
16
NRDC, 16, 88, 113

Mead, Margaret, 113
Mead, Reservoir, 5
Metropolitan Water District of Southern California, 68–70
Mexico
    Public Security Agency in, 92
    Treaty of Guadalupe Hidalgo and, 7
    See also Rio Grande River
Milagro Beanfield War (Nichols), 87
milk dairies. *See* dairies
Mississippi River Valley alluvial aquifer, 23
Missouri Farm Bureau, 80
Missouri River
    Army Corps of Engineers and, 38–42, 76–77, 79–80
    Master Manual for, 41–42, 77–78, 87
    water wars over, 76–81
Muir, John, 63, 65
Mulroy, Pat, 74

N

National Center for Atmospheric Research, 116
National Farmers Union, 36
National Wildlife Federation, 16
Natural Resources Defense Council (NRDC), 16, 88, 113
Navajo Nation, 5–6
New York City
    Catskills and, 83–84, 86
    EPA and, 84
    water sources for, 83–86
Nichols, John, 87
Niobrara River, 24
Northern Rocky Mountains Intermontane Basins aquifer system, 23

Northwest Ordinance (1787), xi
NRDC (Natural Resources Defense Council), 16, 88, 113

O

Ogallala Aquifer, xii, 18–19, 23–24
    agricultural subsidies' relation to, 34
    dairies' relation to, 26–27
    depletion of, 28–29
    food-processing plants' effects on, 27–28
    formation of, 21
    geographic location of, 21
    pollution of, 25–28
    rates of use for, 22
    sustainability of, 30–31
    water conservation measures for, 25, 31–33
    water levels in, 20–22
100th meridian, 43, 54, 172n8
Oregon Trail, xix
organizations, environmental. *See* environmental organizations
O'Shaughnessy Dam, 63–64
    Sierra Club and, 65
Owens River, 66
Owens Valley (CA), 65–67, 87
    EPA in, 66–67
    Owens River in, 66

P

Pacific Northwest basin-fill aquifer, 23
Pahrump Valley Times, 73
"paper water," 7
Parker Dam, 68
Pecos River Basin alluvial aquifer, 23

U

UN. *See* United Nations
unconsolidated-deposit aquifers (AK), 23
Union of Concerned Scientists, xviii
United Nations (UN), 112
　IPCC under, 117
　WHO and, 93
United States
　agricultural subsidies in, 34, 46–51, 53, 54, 56
　agriculture in, 36–56
　American Farm Bureau Federation, 36
　Army Corps of Engineers, 38–42, 46–47, 49, 76–80, 87
　Bill of Rights, x
　Bureau of the Census, 128
　Bureau of Land Management, 46–47, 49, 173n3
　Bureau of Reclamation, 46–47, 49, 62, 72
　"cheap food policy" in, 50, 53
　Endangered Species Act, 77
　EPA, 66–67, 84, 110–11, 130, 140–41, 152
　Farm Bill, 46
　Fish and Wildlife Service, 40–41, 77
　Great Pond Ordinance, xi
　High Plains area, 19–29, 125–26
　Northwest Ordinance, xi
　100th meridian, 43
　Raker Act, 64
　Raker Bill, 64
　Safe Drinking Water Act, 107, 112
　Treaty of Guadalupe Hidalgo and, 7, 10–11
　USDA in, 36–37, 49
　U.S. Mayors Climate Protection Agreement, 127
　water wars in, xxii–xxiii, 58–59, 76–81
　See also agricultural subsidies; agriculture; Arizona; Army Corps of Engineers, U.S.; Atlanta (GA); California; Colorado River; Great Plains; Las Vegas; Los Angeles; Missouri River; Phoenix (AZ); Rio Grande River; San Francisco; Stockton (CA)
United States Department of Agriculture (USDA), 36–37
　agricultural subsidies and, 49
USDA. *See* United States Department of Agriculture
U.S. Mayors Climate Protection Agreement, 127

V

Ventria Rice Company, 122
Veolia Water, 99, 104, 110
Vivendi, 110

W

water
　"beneficial use" appropriation of, 14
　bottled, xviii

water (*continued*)
   contamination of, xvii–xviii
   in food-processing plants,
      xxi
   in hydrologic cycle,
      xxiii–xxiv
   privatization of, 92–113
   reverse osmosis and, 93–95,
      137, 141–42
   shortages of, xviii, 45,
      123–28
   transportation of, 143–57,
      162
   See also dams; desalination;
      groundwater pumping;
      privatization; water con-
      servation; water rights;
      water transportation;
      water wars
water bladders, 155–56
waterborne contamination. *See*
   contamination, waterborne
water conservation
   along Rio Grande River, 15
   for Ogallala Aquifer, 25,
      31–33
water distillation, 137–38
Water Environment Federation,
   98
Water Follies (Glennon), 151
water rights
   "paper," 7
   political influences on, 165
   for Rio Grande River, 8–11
   "wet," 7

water shortages, xviii
   agricultural effects from, 45
   from global warming,
      123–28
water transportation
   by aqueducts, 143–44
   by bladders, 155–56
   Central Arizona Project and,
      144
   by groundwater pumping,
      148–52, 162
   icebergs and, 152–57, 162
   by pipeline, 143–48
   See also groundwater pump-
      ing
water wars, xxii–xxiii, 58–89
   over Missouri River, 76–81
"welfare queens," rice companies
   as, 56
We, the Living (Whitten), 37
"wet water," 7
Whitten, James, 37
WHO (World Health
   Organization), 93
Willamette Lowland basin-fill
   aquifers, 23
Wilson, Woodrow, 63
wind energy, 133
Woodall, Angela, 96, 99
Woolrych, Henry William, xi
World Bank, ix
World Health Organization
   (WHO), 93
World Water Forum, 92

ABOUT THE AUTHOR

There was a creek running through the front yard of Ken Midkiff's childhood home in western Kentucky. There were other sources of water — a deep well that had been drilled in search of oil and a hand-dug well just outside the back door of the farmhouse.

In late summer, the creek would dry up. Particularly dry years would lower the water table below the level of the hand-dug well. That would leave one source of water — the deep well where oil was not found, but water was. Not only did all the animals of the Midkiff farm depend on that water — which had to be pumped by hand — but neighbors came and filled up their barrels as their sources dried up.

From that experience, Midkiff knows all too well the danger of running out of water. He knows firsthand what it means when the well runs dry and the only water available is difficult to access.

In 1994, after multiple careers ranging from serving as an assistant to the Illinois superintendent of education to owning and operating a fishing and vacation resort on Missouri's Table Rock Lake, Midkiff became the director of the Sierra Club in Missouri and subsequently, the director of the Sierra Club's Clean Water Campaign. After stepping down as a staff member of the Sierra Club, Midkiff wrote *The Meat You Eat* (St. Martin's Press, 2004) and embarked on a national tour to promote that book.

Midkiff lives in Columbia, Missouri, with his wife, Julie. He has two children, Mike and Charlie, and three grandchildren, Simon, Eben, and Chloe. In spite of all this domesticity, Midkiff hiked the Appalachian Trail and the Ozark Trail in recent years. He is an avid camper, canoeist, bicyclist, and hiker.

New World Library is dedicated to publishing books and other media that inspire and challenge us to improve the quality of our lives and the world.

We are a socially and environmentally aware company, and we strive to embody the ideals presented in our publications. We recognize that we have an ethical responsibility to our customers, our staff members, and our planet.

We serve our customers by creating the finest publications possible on personal growth, creativity, spirituality, wellness, and other areas of emerging importance. We serve New World Library employees with generous benefits, significant profit sharing, and constant encouragement to pursue their most expansive dreams.

As a member of the Green Press Initiative, we print an increasing number of books with soy-based ink on 100 percent postconsumer-waste recycled paper. Also, we power our offices with solar energy and contribute to nonprofit organizations working to make the world a better place for us all.

Our products are available
in bookstores everywhere.
For our catalog, please contact:

New World Library
14 Pamaron Way
Novato, California 94949

Phone: 415-884-2100 or 800-972-6657
Catalog requests: Ext. 50
Orders: Ext. 52
Fax: 415-884-2199
Email: escort@newworldlibrary.com

To subscribe to our electronic newsletter, visit
www.newworldlibrary.com